On Cukor

ON CUKOR

Gavin Lambert

G. P. PUTNAM'S SONS *New York*

To Don Bachardy

ACKNOWLEDGMENTS

THE research for this book was sponsored by the American Film Institute as part of the Louis B. Mayer Oral History Fund. The original tapes are now in the institute's library in Beverly Hills, California. I am also grateful for the institute's patience in tracing rare prints of films for me to see and to Daniel Selznick, who allowed me to screen prints from the Selznick collection.

Illustrations: Paramount Pictures, the Selznick Studio, M-G-M, Columbia, Universal, Twentieth Century-Fox, Warner Brothers, and George Cukor.

Contents

CONTENTS

On Cukor

Introduction

THESE CONVERSATIONS with George Cukor were tape-recorded at his Hollywood home during several months in 1970. In editing them, I have aimed at a portrait with background. The figure is framed in a Hollywood landscape. Beyond the films themselves, and his feelings about them, is Hollywood as it's evolved over the last forty years; thoughts on his craft; memories, friendships, impressions; people and events that have fascinated, saddened, influenced and disappointed him. The man who has given most of his life to making movies (almost fifty of them) has also managed to live in a very personal, independent and, for the most part, satisfied way. The life and the work have been partners, and surprisingly happy ones.

There are artists whose work is basically a release from personal tension, and there are others for whom their work is an extension rather than a tension, a mode of pleasure and a way of expressing curiosity about the world. Cukor is of the second kind. It may sound easier than the first, but its cornerstones are the same: discipline, alertness, energy. He works like a transmitter, the current passes through him, to his antennae, and so to his audience. He is not a confessional film maker, like Fellini, or a polemical one, like Bunuel. Looking for a single word to describe both the

[1]

work and the life, I think "discreet" is the best. It implies delicacy, prudence and something enigmatic. In making his films, and in talking about them, Cukor's first instinct is to *defer*—to his actors, his writers, and so on. The "I" exists but doesn't care to advertise itself.

When somebody important enters a room, the effect may be so grand that you overlook whoever opened the door—a mistake when that door and others were opened by Cukor. If he hadn't shown the way, the room itself would not have been there.

The house, like its owner, is elevated and private. Outside, a high wall discloses practically nothing. The gate doesn't open until you've announced yourself on a telephone set in the wall; then an electronic device buzzes approval and the handle yields to your touch. Inside, a private world begins immediately. It's as sudden as opening the door of a sound stage and finding yourself on a lighted set. You enter a neat, extensive and brilliant garden —terraces, statues, a summer house, a swimming pool and fountains of constantly trickling water. A flight of steps leads up to the house, Southern California Mediterranean, reminiscent of those villas in Cannes and Nice that stand rather aloof today from the hotels that have sprung up since.

The interior is spacious but not intimidating. It manages to combine luxury and comfort, orderliness and relaxation. There are many paintings—by Matisse, Picasso, Braque, Sutherland—a Rodin bronze, a Tchelitchew drawing, a portrait of Ethel Barrymore by Sargent. And memorabilia everywhere. In one hallway the walls teem with photographs of friends, Artur Rubinstein, Vivien Leigh, Katharine Hepburn, David Selznick, Garbo, Ava Gardner, the Gish sisters as kiddies, the young and stunningly beautiful Gladys Cooper. On a desk in the library stands an inscribed photograph of John F. Kennedy, and on a special shelf a row of books inscribed by their authors, who include Thomas Mann, Aldous Huxley, Christopher Isherwood, Somerset Maugham, Edith Sitwell (*The Queens and the Hive* is also dedicated to him), Anita Loos and Sinclair Lewis. However, after many visits to the house, it was only recently that I noticed where Cukor keeps his *My Fair Lady* Oscar. It's placed among some books on a fairly remote high shelf, as casually set as the swimming pool in the garden outside.

Supremely well run and staffed without making a point of it, this house is one of those rare affluent sanctuaries that exist for the personal enjoyment of its owner. You have the feeling that it has grown up around him, keeping pace with his life. Puritans will be at once on guard. "If he lives that well, he can't be serious." Others, who agree with Montaigne that it's better to live happily rather than die happily, will be delighted and at ease, like the owner himself.

Born a few months before the twentieth century, he is a man of medium height and solid, stocky build. The hair is silvery, the features sharp as perfect projection on a movie screen. Movements, gestures and eyes all give the same impression: a contained but constantly flowing energy, like the fountains outside. The mouth, thickly lipped, opens and closes like a trap. The hands dart and swoop. When he laughs, which is often, everything seems to gleam. He retires and rises early, doesn't smoke, drinks very little (a Dubonnet, sometimes two, before dinner) and was born under Cancer. This is the sign of quiet tenaciousness, of the teacher and lover of objects, of patience, adaptability and the pronounced jaw.

In recent years he's made fewer films. Various projects, like many other people's, have failed to materialize. Since *My Fair Lady* in 1964 he has directed only *Justine*, taken over after shooting began and only fitfully his own. None of this slows him down. Aspiring young actors and actresses come to see him and are given advice; directors visiting from Europe are invited to lunch. He has a great appetite for new movies, seeing almost everything that promises to be interesting, and being particularly delighted by the Fellini *Satyricon* and Paul Morrissey's *Trash, Stolen Kisses* and *The Sicilian Clan*. At the University of Southern California, where he has endowed a graduate fellowship, he is very active in an organization called Friends of the Libraries. It gives dinner testimonials to various people in the arts, tending to specialize in those who have recently died. (A flamboyant exception is Mae West.) Cukor has masterminded, behind the scenes and on the podium, several of these. For recollections of his old friend Somerset Maugham he brought together Garson Kanin, Ruth Gordon and Clare Boothe Luce, for a tribute to another friend, Aldous Huxley, he appeared with Laura Huxley and Christopher Isherwood, and to honor Vivien Leigh ("I consider myself blessed to

Early gesture. Cukor
age five.

Later gesture. Cukor at the
door to his home.

"Fat" film: Cukor directs Garbo in *Camille,* 1937

"Thin" film: Cukor with Cary Grant on the set of
The Philadelphia Story, 1940

have known her") he assembled a large group of friends and colleagues. None of which implies withdrawal from the present, simply a concern that the past be given its due. I should note, in this connection, his scrupulous attendance at the funerals of friends, which he describes as "my kind of religion," and his supervision of a three-and-one-half-hour-long anthology film called *The Movies.* Made to be shown at benefit performances for the Motion Picture and Television Relief Fund, it begins with early Griffith and Chaplin and ends with *2001.* Subtitled *A Colossal Compilation of Extraordinary Excerpts from the Seventy-Year Span of American Cinema,* it offers along the way such unexpected treasures as the record of a publicity luncheon at the M-G-M commissary in the forties, with Louis B. Mayer presiding over a fantastic, gone-forever roll call of stars.

Cukor's social life is conducted with a kind of intense discrimination. He avoids most of the big bashes and concentrates on small dinner parties, sometimes organizing one for a special occasion, such as the now legendary meeting of Garbo and Mae West. Any public function of which he disapproves, such as a studio reception for Madame Ngu while he was shooting *My Fair Lady,* will be firmly refused. A contrast: he drives a Rolls-Royce and is devoted to an aging, refreshingly unbeautified standard black poodle.

"The green light" is a Hollywood term for the moment when the studio approves a project. Toward the end of our talks, Cukor received it from M-G-M for an adaptation of Graham Greene's *Travels with My Aunt,* his ninth film with Katharine Hepburn. The motors began whirring with characteristic intensity. One example of the passion for detail: departing for Europe to look at locations, he was particularly concerned to find the "right" English crematorium. (An important scene takes place there.) He visited more than a dozen before discovering one that truly satisfied him.

In an article on Cukor for *Holiday* magazine, Kenneth Tynan quoted from a letter by Lesley Blanch: "I think he has not, or has passed, *ambition,* in the destructive sense. This makes him utterly free. And being perfectly sure of who he is, what he is, he does not envy—is not eaten up by competition." However, it's characteristic of people who really know who and what they are that they find it unnecessary to announce the fact. As a result, Cukor's work has puzzled those who expect an immediate signature on a film and imagine there is no "personality" behind it unless they can make the response of Hitchcock-suspense, Bunuel-surrealism, Fellini-grotesquerie, and so on. Even Tynan, in the *Holiday* article, can only come up with the comment that Cukor's films "epitomize Hollywood at its most stylish." (Why not "Cukor at his most stylish"?) The "Hollywood" label is an example of several meaningless ones that have haunted Cukor's career, some of the others being "women's director," "glossy entertainment" and "essentially theatrical." And yet the films themselves dispel category-mongering. The "women's director" discovered Cary Grant as a romantic comedian in *Sylvia Scarlett*, launched the movie careers of Jack Lemmon and Aldo Ray, guided W. C. Fields and John Barrymore to their best performances in *David Copperfield* and *Dinner at Eight* and James Stewart, Ronald Colman and Rex Harrison to Oscars. Some of his most individual films are *Little Women*, *The Marrying Kind*, *Pat and Mike* and *Bhowani Junction*. None of them is glossy, and none of them derived from the theater.

All of which produces another misunderstanding. If Cukor can't be labeled, it must be because he's the kind of director who takes on all types of assignments and executes them as best he can, without deep personal involvement. Setting aside the question "How well can you execute anything without personal involvement?" this point of view seems to imply something undesirable in a wide range of subjects. Since no one questions Renoir when he moves from India to seventeenth-century Peru to France past and present, it has to be a matter of fashion. Renoir's talent has been rightly acknowledged for a long time, so we're accustomed to locating it wherever he chooses to set it. Cukor has not yet received his due, so the perfect Americana of *Little Women*, the relentless middle-class accuracy of *The Marrying Kind*, the romanticism of *Camille*, the Park Avenue elegance of *Holiday* are looked at not for themselves, as personal achievements, but become theoretical "cases" of individuality submerged by too great a range of subjects.

While French movie critics may go overboard in their admiration for Raoul Walsh or Douglas Sirk, they've always looked at films without literary preconceptions, and their hits are as good as their misses. From Jean-George Auriol in the '30's to Truffaut and Eric Rohmer before they became directors, they were the first to appreciate the extent of Hitchcock's art and the first to discover Cukor's. It may be helpful to show what this nonliterary way of looking at movies implies. From a play based entirely on verbal wit, *Lady Windermere's Fan*, Lubitsch could make a silent film not only as witty but less creaky than the original. Hitchcock in his whole work has used devices that would seem crude or ridiculous in a novel or play, creating a world in which outrageous coincidences seem inevitable and sometimes beautiful, as well as throwing a new light on "reality." In *Lonesome Cowboys*, Andy Warhol revives the improvised adventure of early silent pictures, "happenings" in which theatrical construction (plot, development, climax) is thrown out for the joy of informality and casual surprise. All this is another way of saying sometimes you can only discover what is being done by how it's being done. The best way to the cause, more often than not, is through the effect.

Reviewing *David Copperfield* at the time (1935), Jean-George Auriol immediately spotted, from *watching what was happening on the screen*, that Cukor was not simply an extraordinary director of actors but "an artist and a creator, equally at ease in reconstructing middle-class interiors of a hundred years ago, in staging a shipwreck or creating a fairy-tale image." And Truffaut in his critic days saw in the (more or less) potboiler of *A Life of Her Own* the same "beauty" of work as in *Holiday* or *Little Women*. When the Cinémathèque Française showed a retrospective of Cukor's films a few years ago, Henri Langlois summed up their appeal as "*knowledge of the world*—elegance of style, distinction of subjects chosen, distinction of actors, refinement of cutting, a world in which everything is in half-tones, suggested and never over-stressed." Two things occur here. "Content" is seen as no more important than what the director does with it, and—once again—the qualities admired hardly conform to the image of Cukor as manufacturer of popular entertainment or superior artisan of M-G-M.

It is completely in character that Cukor should be reluctant to think of himself as an *auteur*, which is a hateful word anyway, and that he prefers to decline the crown. He dislikes crowns, theories, editorials, self-advertisement, anything else that suggests arrogance or pretentiousness. Nothing is more quintessential Cukor than *Pat and Mike*, that comedy without a belly laugh, that love story without an embrace. In the same way, he is attracted to *Gaslight* as a melodrama with no visible act of violence and to *The Actress*, whose story ends before she ever appears on the stage. No accident, either, that his admiration for Warhol and Morrissey is returned, because Cukor's whole career is a fine example of contemporary virtues. He's done his thing and kept his cool, he has never moralized or intruded on his subjects. Yet they remain *his*, and no one else's.

During one of our talks, quoted in this book, Cukor remarks that "anyone who looks at something special in a very original way, makes you see it that way forever." He will always, he says, see the South Seas through Maugham's eyes, and a row of plane trees beside a river in France the way post-Impressionists painted them. And this is what Cukor's own art is about. I know that he has fixed for me the texture of New England life, its stern charm and austere optimism, in *Little Women* and *The Actress;* at a different moment in time, he creates the definitive picture of those pre-World War Two rich families in *Holiday* and *The Philadelphia Story*, luxuriously trapped by selfishness and charm; with Garbo, he suggests in *Camille* the "champagne and tears" of Bohemian life in Paris as no other film has done; in *The Marrying Kind*, an "ordinary" American marriage becomes extraordinary, precariously balanced between the tragic and the trivial; and if I ever go to India, I shall expect the "grandeur and exposed electric wires" of *Bhowani Junction*.

Some directors reveal themselves through a single world. Others, like Cukor, through several worlds.

The style with which Cukor creates these different worlds has the great virtue of *rightness* in relation to its subject. To existing forms he brings a strong yet subtle freshness. During the fifties the location work on his New York pictures *(Adam's Rib, Pat and Mike, The Marrying Kind, It Should Happen to You)* went almost unnoticed. Seeing them again today, you wonder at the critical fuss over similar methods in *Midnight Cowboy*, accomplished but superficial. The Cukor films have a powerful documentary quality and at times (in *Pat and Mike* and *The Marrying Kind*) crossbreed fantasy and reality in a very original way; but the style was so unadvertised that hardly anyone commented on it. Again, in *A Star Is Born*, the dramatic use of the Cinema-Scope screen—the only truly successful approach to that unfortunate shape—the hand-held camera scenes and quick, nervous, against-the-rules cutting seemed too naturally effective for praise. In this sense Cukor works like Renoir. Seeing again an early Renoir such as *Bondu Sauvé des Eaux* (1932), you are astonished not only at its "contemporary" tone, the ruthless black humor of a middle-class family trying to befriend a dropout and make him respectable, but at the way stylistic effects are taken for granted and almost thrown away—extreme depth of focus, shooting in actual interiors as well as exteriors, some dolly shots as elaborate as Max Ophuls'. "Technique," Renoir once said, "that's a terrible word in art! You have to have it, but so completely that you know how to disguise it."

Another clue to this style is Cukor's treatment of the past. He approaches it as if it were the present. It is *still there*. The Paris of *Camille*, Dickens' England in *David Copperfield*, New England during the Civil War in *Little Women*, the pioneer West in *Heller in Pink Tights*—none of these is self-consciously "reconstructed" but comes as directly and immediately alive as Judy Holliday and Aldo Ray walking in Central Park or Judy Garland as the unknown Esther Blodgett arriving at the studio in *A Star Is Born*. This is a very special gift, making dramatic contact with whatever reality faces him, and Cukor does it through a combination of his own sensibilities and imaginative research. Even when the material is spurious, as in *A Life of Her Own*, there is nothing perfunctory or tricked-up about the work itself. Too candid to make you believe in something false, it is shrewd enough to suggest (as Cukor likes to say about his movies that have dated) a reality beyond the convention.

Cukor approaches his characters in the same way, without any bias except his belief in them. Three of his films contain remarkable sequences of the disintegration of a man: John Barrymore in *Dinner at Eight* and James Mason in *A Star Is Born* before they commit suicide, Aldo Ray in *The Marrying Kind* when Judy Holliday leaves him. There is nothing solemn about any of them (the Barrymore scene is done with ironic humor) and no "dramatic" camera angles or visual effects. Emotion is concentrated on what the actor is doing, on a totally personal response. Cukor says about Mason in *A Star Is Born* that it was "a case of letting him find things out for himself." It's as if the director knows exactly when to perform an act of inspired withdrawal and let the moment take over.

Psychophysiological note: "I once said, my chief claim to fame will be that I once lost seventy-two pounds, and I fired Bette Davis," Cukor remarked during one of our talks. Not the least dramatic aspect of this book's many illustrations of the director at work is the weight problem. Soon after his arrival in Hollywood, the silhouette becomes almost Hitchcockian, and most of the thirties films are "fat"—*Dinner at Eight, Little Women, David Copperfield, Romeo and Juliet, Sylvia Scarlett, Camille, Holiday* and *The Women*. After *The Women* a drastic reduction occurs, and a "thin" cycle begins—*The Philadelphia Story, Her Cardboard Lover, Two-Faced Woman, Keeper of the Flame, Gaslight*. The pounds return toward the end of the forties, beginning with *A Double Life*, and *Adam's Rib, The Marrying Kind* and the other films written by Garson Kanin and Ruth Gordon are "semifat." *A Star Is Born* announces a new cycle, the "semithin" or "solid." The face becomes progressively leaner and sharper, and the body settles into its natural contours. Under the guidance of a physical instructor, he becomes notably fit and healthy, a final period which happily continues.

Somerset Maugham once remarked that "to write good prose is an affair of good manners." (Strange that it should have been the one thing he found almost impossible, as a writer, to do.) Cukor feels the same way about making films well. At certain points these two artists coincide. Supreme professionals, they are lucid, curious and prolific. Like Maugham, Cukor enjoys his profession. Then, beyond this, they part. His friend always seemed to write out of some concealed affliction. Cukor directs, and lives, with open delight. For him the cinema is an art of pleasure, worldly, perceptive, humorous and discreetly sensual. And when he talks about forty years of preoccupation with it, the result is an expression of that expression.

On Being (and Not Being) an *Auteur*

CUKOR: I'm not an *auteur*, alas. And the whole *auteur* theory disconcerts me. To begin with, damn few directors can write. I have too much respect for good writers to think of taking over that job. Also, to be frank, not all directors can direct. Recently there was a big, very successful picture called *Patton*. It would have been a hell of a lot better—in the battle scenes, and in the performances, too—with a really experienced professional director like Henry Hathaway. He'd have given it that much more color and variety.

LAMBERT: So what you find basically wrong with *Patton* is the direction, not the script. Doesn't that suggest the director is the key factor after all?

CUKOR: Are you going to try and persuade me that I'm an *auteur*?

LAMBERT: Yes.

CUKOR (*amused*): Well . . . I thought what I was saying was, you don't have to be some kind of a Renaissance man, it's enough to be a good director. You have to know what you can do a little better than somebody else, and you have to think of your limita-

Expressions of a director: with Virginia Grey and
Joan Crawford on *The Women*

tions. Of course, there are unexplored facets in a director. Offhand, I'd never say I was just the boy to direct a Western, but
with *Heller in Pink Tights* I thought I made a damned interesting try. There are certain things you're antipathetic to, and that
shows on the screen just as much as the things you care for.

LAMBERT: You say you're not an *auteur* because you don't
write your own scripts—but aren't there two kinds of *auteurs*? I
don't think the theory means anything at all, really, but let's stick
with it for a moment. There's the *auteur*-director, who writes his
own scripts, alone or in collaboration with somebody else, like
Fellini or Welles or Bunuel or Bergman. There's the director
who doesn't write his own scripts but certainly influences them,
like Hitchcock or Von Sternberg or Lubitsch. This is where I
think you come in. Either way, no one can deny that the films
which result have a personal style and personal imagination. Does
it really matter whether a director actually writes his own script or

not, whether he was assigned to make a picture or whether he set it up himself? Doesn't the whole theory break down under any sort of practical scrutiny? And aren't we really talking about the same thing? A director either has ideas and a style different from anyone else's, or he hasn't.

CUKOR (*a bit won over*): Well . . . Griffith never had a script, of course. He kept it all in his head. He was a real *auteur*, he conceived the whole thing and controlled it. (*Doubtful again*) But he *did* conceive the whole thing. I don't *conceive* my pictures like that. Perhaps because I came originally from the theater, I rely a great deal on the script.

LAMBERT: But are you bound by the script?

CUKOR: No, it sustains me and frees me at the same time.

LAMBERT: And you approach each film in your own way.

CUKOR: We all see things at a certain slant.

LAMBERT: Let's take some pictures you've made that are very different in their subject matter—*Little Women, Gaslight, Pat and Mike, Bhowani Junction*. You made each of them in your own way, and it's completely different from anyone else's.

CUKOR: I'm not aware of that. It happens, I suppose. But I really don't know what the process is. I suppose I influence a great deal in many ways. I have ideas about the script, I influence the performances very much, and visually I go on a great deal about sets and clothes. Yet I'm not a writer or a designer or a cameraman.

LAMBERT: But you *are* the one who says very firmly, "I want that, I don't want that, that looks right, that looks wrong, I believe that"—

CUKOR: Yes! (*Emphatic*) That's very important. That, I choose to say, is style. You make big decisions and small decisions and decisions you aren't even consciously aware of. You do unexpected things on the set. You have a vision. . . . Yes, I suppose a director influences everything. But what about directors who collaborate with writers on the script? That's all very mysterious to me. You see this other name on the script credit, and you don't know who the hell he is, and maybe *he's* the real backroom influence on the whole thing?

LAMBERT: On each Antonioni film you see a string of names on the script credit. Except for Antonioni's, they're different every time—but each film is unmistakably his.

[14]

CUKOR: Yes. (*Doubtful again*) Maybe what sticks in my craw is the physical writing of the thing. I could never undertake to write a scene. I can only have suggestions that work or don't work. (*More firmly*) I know that I always want the best, the greatest help, the best writers, cutters, designers and actors. And that doesn't always mean the most celebrated ones.

LAMBERT: You have a great talent for knowing who the best are. You've launched a lot of new actors—Katharine Hepburn, Angela Lansbury, Jack Lemmon, Aldo Ray, Judy Holliday. And a lot of others—Garbo and Judy Garland and Spencer Tracy— have been at their absolute best in your movies. You discovered Gene Allen as an art director, and you collaborated with George Hoyningen-Huene as a kind of color experimenter—

CUKOR: Yes, it interests me to find new people and discover new facets in them—you can help them to discover things in themselves. You dig, dig, dig, and you discover things. I suppose that's a contribution.

LAMBERT: And in all of this your curiosity is a very important factor.

CUKOR: I'm full of curiosity! And I have an almost mystic respect for other people's talent. When I worked with Hoyningen-Huene, who was a very distinguished photographer in his own right, I would express some ideas, and he'd listen and sometimes say "No." Because we respected each other, there was no problem. Very often his disagreement helped and freed me. There's no such thing as absolute freedom. You have freedom within the context of what you're doing and what you're able to do. Too often today it's sheer egomania when a new director wants to do everything—produce the picture, write the script and the music, and so on. I notice some of them are very tough about billing, too; they certainly get their names up there on top, all over the place. Curiously enough, their work often has many of the vices of the old school but too few of the virtues. I am forced to suspect that much of this talk about "integrity" and "freedom" is far from pure. Once in a while, of course, someone like Fellini comes along and really carries the whole film in his head, as Griffith used to. But I've seen him being interviewed on TV, and he strikes me as a genuinely modest man. He's not snide about "Hollywood," he doesn't set himself up as a "revolutionary" and so on, and try

... with Garbo on *Two-Faced Woman*

... with Norma Shearer on *Her Cardboard Lover*

... with Aldo Ray
and Judy Holliday
on *The Marrying
Kind*

... with Ray Danton
and Shelley Winters
on *The Chapman
Report*

. . . with Audrey Hepburn on *My Fair Lady*

to tear everything else down. Knowing what you can do is part of knowing yourself. All the rest is just boasting and reveals an ungenerous spirit. It doesn't result in the best picture making, either.

LAMBERT: You seem to have a very simple, practical definition of freedom, which is: When you decide to make a movie and you want to make it in a certain way, the management allows you to do so.

CUKOR: Yes, professionally I think just this: once I've been given the agreement on certain things—very crucial things, casting, and sometimes on the script—I've found that I've been allowed a great deal of freedom as a director and received a great deal of encouragement. It's very rarely that I remember the studio saying, "Oh, we don't like the way you're doing this." But sometimes, when the whole thing is over, it's been a different story. Everybody expertises too much about the cutting and so on. Even so, although not every picture has gone the way I hoped, I've had a good record of working with intelligent producers. Everything can't always go the way you hope, anyway. I've learned how to function within what they call the system. I can only say that for me it's had certain disadvantages but also enormous virtues. Mind you, for a great deal of the time that I've been making pictures, the system has functioned well. When it doesn't, as nowadays, it's a different story.

LAMBERT: You once told me that people come to you and say how they admire this and this picture you've made—and then proceed to attack the Hollywood system. And you've had to remind them, these pictures they like were made within the system.

CUKOR: It's true. All my films that people have written about, and in some cases been mad about, were made within the system. I hate this gloating that Hollywood is supposed to be dead. Some wretched young man comes to see me and then writes a piece about how Hollywood is dead. . . . Well, like the theater, it's a "Fabulous Invalid" and it's always dying. Or always changing. Recently a journalist from some magazine came to interview me, and of course he began talking about all the changes here, and how terrible things were. So I asked him to show me a copy of his magazine, and I looked at it, and then I said, "Oh, yes, I remember that magazine when it used to be a great big fat magazine. Now it's quite slim, only a few pages. Well, everything changes."

LAMBERT: I like very much something that Katharine Hepburn said about you. She said she used to wish you'd put more of a stamp, your own stamp, on things. But then she thought, "No, I don't. You never had to put a label on the bottle, because it was unmistakable. All the people in your pictures are as goddamned good as they can possibly be, and that's your stamp."

Beginnings

CUKOR: I'm lost in admiration for people who come to New York or Hollywood with no money, only hopes. I had the enormous advantage of being born in New York and living at home when I first went out to fend for jobs in the theater. And later I came to Hollywood because I'd been offered a job there. My parents weren't rich but there were moderately well off—a Hungarian family, my grandfather arrived in America in the seventies, at a time when there was very little Hungarian immigration. My uncle became a successful lawyer, he was the lawyer for the Austro-Hungarian Embassy, and I had another uncle, a bachelor who was very generous with us. We were a very close-knit family, and my sister and I were the only grandchildren. It was generally hoped I'd become a lawyer, but I was fascinated by the theater from the time I was twelve. My parents used to go to the Irving Place Theatre—a German theater—and my mother, who, like all Hungarian immigrants of a certain education, was trilingual, speaking German, Hungarian and English, she explained to me that while the German immigrants of that time were good, solid people, butchers and artisans and so on, it was the *Hungarians* who supported this theater, who were really literate. . . . I'm surprised to this day how much I learned and absorbed as a child. I wasn't much good at school, and I graduated none too gloriously, but I've always found that I know a lot more than I thought I knew—historical facts and so on. We were not a religious family, but when I saw the movie of *The Bible* a few years ago I was amazed at how much I remembered—all those *names*. They must have been taught me at some time. . . .

LAMBERT: When did you decide you didn't want to be a lawyer?

CUKOR: After I graduated from high school. I said to my family, "I want to go into the theater." Nothing can shock parents today, of course, but then it was as if I'd said, "Well, Mom and Dad, I'm going to become a pusher." I didn't know at first exactly what I wanted to do in the theater, but I said to myself, "I want to be a director." Probably I didn't have the courage to want to be an actor. I didn't really know what a director was.

LAMBERT: How about movies? Were you aware of them at this time?

CUKOR: Yes, but people were very snooty about movies in those days. I remember my sister's sister-in-law saying, "There was the strangest man who gave a lecture and showed this movie." Its title was *Birth of a Nation*. Later on, in sixteen and seventeen, I used to go to the 68th Street Playhouse, rather a tatty little place then but an art theater now, and I saw several Griffith movies. My family wasn't highbrow, but I had some highbrow friends, two brothers, very musical, one of them an expert on fifteenth-century Florentine art. Their mother had this weakness for movies, and they thought it rather funny. She bought movie magazines, which is how I read them for the first time. Later, when she was very ill, her own life faded away and she lived in the world of the movies she'd seen—they were more real than her life, her children, everything she'd lived through. (That's a quality that movies have.) But the theater was what fascinated me.

LAMBERT: Did you go to a lot of plays?

CUKOR: Two or three times a week! I saw everything—from the second balcony. How the hell I got away from school I don't know, but I seem to remember my family being very easygoing

In the garden: with Tallulah Bankhead, 1931

In the garden: with Merle Oberon and Sir Alexander Korda, 1941

about it. And I saw New York theater at a marvelous period. I was right at the hub of it.

LAMBERT: What are the stand-out memories of that time?

CUKOR: There was a man called Arthur Hopkins, originally a newspaper man, who became a great director in the theater. His productions were neither slick nor expensive, and all the things that other people did very well, he did rather awkwardly and didn't care about. The plays he chose always had literary merit, and he developed his own method of directing. First of all, he would just rehearse the play and say nothing at all. He'd rehearse again and again, concentrating on the text. In his presence actors began to discard the tricks they'd learned, and the play itself would emerge without any artificial aids. He created a wonderfully exciting theater, doing plays by O'Neill and Philip Barry, including *In a Garden* with Laurette Taylor and *Hamlet* with John Barrymore. For this he worked with the designer Robert Edmond Jones, and they introduced a whole new look into the theater, experimenting with color and lighting effects. He was even the first director to discard the use of footlights. His work really electrified me, and I learned a great deal from it.

LAMBERT: The method you describe—coming face-to-face with the material—became very much your own.

CUKOR: Then I saw all the Barrymores in their heyday, of course, and Laurette Taylor in several plays, and Yvette Guilbert, and Isadora Duncan, and the Diaghilev Ballet. All these things left their mark on me. (And some of these people I later got to know and work with. When I worked with the Barrymores, the residue remained of having first seen them from the second balcony.) I saw everything, good and bad, and it educated me. I learned about acting and was sensitive to speech and style. I read a lot of plays, too, the public library was full of Pinero and Sutro and Shaw, although Shaw didn't attract me much then. I learned all about England from those plays.

LAMBERT: What was your first job?

CUKOR: Assistant stage manager in New York, and then in Chicago for something called *The Better Ole*. I went on tour with this on one-night stands. Then I came back to New York and went around the agencies to look for something else. In those days lots of people used to make the rounds—I met a young man called Moss Hart, who was employed as secretary to a theatrical man-

ager. I got other assistant jobs, and then I became a damn good
stage manager. I managed a show for the Selwyns, a big theatrical company at that time. Being a stage manager is very good
experience, because once a play has opened you have to keep it
up to scratch. And there are things which aren't purely mechanical—the ringing down of the curtain at the exact moment, the
tempo at which it comes down. You also conduct understudy
rehearsals.

LAMBERT: What kind of plays did the Selwyns produce?

CUKOR: They did a play by Somerset Maugham—which is how
I first met him. The play, which has never been published, was a
kind of farce. It didn't do very well, and they made some rather
ruthless cuts in it. So I was disloyal to my employers and went and
told Maugham about them, and he said, "If-if-if you write easily,
it really doesn't matter!" I think maybe this was the beginning of
my friendship with him. I remember that his commonsense attitude to the cuts made a deep impression on me. Throughout his
life Maugham was always extremely practical, and if you have
horse sense you're likely to spare yourself a lot of griefs. You'll
also survive, incidentally. A lot of very talented people don't have
horse sense, and they suffer. But Maugham had it to a supreme
degree, and Moss Hart, too. (Ethel Barrymore used to say about
Hart, "He knows the score.") And a third important friend I
made at this time had the same quality, too.

LAMBERT: Who was this?

CUKOR: I'd taken a job as stage manager for a stock company in
Syracuse, New York. They did Broadway plays out of town in the
summer. A dazzlingly pretty girl came to see me; her name was
Frances Howard McLaughlin and she'd been in the chorus of *Oh
Lady, Lady!* and done some modeling for *Vogue* and *Harper's
Bazaar*. Since that first meeting we've been loving and good
friends—for fifty-one years, which is quite something. Not long
after we met she got a big part in a musical called *Wedding Bells*,
and then she married Sam Goldwyn. It was she who introduced
me to Gilbert Miller—

LAMBERT: The theatrical manager?

CUKOR: Yes, but wait a minute. We're jumping ahead. After
Syracuse, I somehow undertook the management of a stock company in Rochester. That's when I began directing plays. If I do
say so, I worked goddamned hard and managed the whole thing

brilliantly. I did everything, I chose the plays and the scenery, I tried out new plays with only one week's rehearsal. Nothing daunted me. We'd do musical comedy one week, then an all-colored play, and so on. I think it was the most exciting stock company in the United States and damned good preparation for Hollywood. The leading man was Louis Calhern and the leading lady Miriam Hopkins.

LAMBERT: Is this the company from which you're supposed to have fired a young unknown called Bette Davis?

CUKOR (*amused*): I once said my chief claim to fame will be that I once lost seventy-two pounds, and I fired Bette Davis. But let me tell you what really happened. This pretty, blond, rather shy girl came to see me, and she'd been working at the Provincetown Theatre in New York. I engaged her to play some minor parts, and the play I was doing at that time was a damned good melodrama called *Broadway*, set backstage in a nightclub. The next part is like the plot of *42d Street*. There's a moment when the villain is alone onstage, and it looks like nothing can stop him, and he's enjoying his triumph. One of the six chorus girls you see from time to time in the play comes quietly down a stairway from the dressing rooms. She takes out a revolver and shoots him. The shot is covered by a burst of music offstage, then she runs back upstairs. You don't know who she is, or why—it's a great *coup de théâtre*. Well, after the Wednesday matinee, the young girl playing this part turned her ankle and couldn't go on. I asked this blond girl, "Do you think you can do it?" and she said, "Yes," and I ran her through it. She had no lines. That night I saw the performance, and she crept downstairs with her baby face and took out the revolver—and suddenly there was Bette Davis! She shot the man with an almost maniacal intensity, she *willed* him dead. . . . We were very impressed and tried to find other parts for her to do, but the season was already set, and the things we asked her to do she was really too young for. . . . Anyway, my partner and I reluctantly decided to let her go. This became a big *histoire*, and to this day Bette Davis is still writing and talking about it.

LAMBERT: Why?

CUKOR: I don't know. (*Amused again*) Imagine, since she became this great tragedienne and important person, I've been constantly reading that she was once fired by George Cukor! Sometimes she says it ironically and sometimes with a kind of self-pity. And I'd really been awfully kind to her. Years later our paths crossed and I said, "Bette, for Christ's sake stop talking about being fired in Rochester, we've all been fired and we'll all be fired again before we're dead," and she laughed, but not long after I read a newspaper interview with her, and I thought, "She can't really still go on about this," but sure enough she could—though this time she did it with humor.

LAMBERT: Well, I read an interview with her last week and she *didn't* mention it.

CUKOR: Oh, good!

LAMBERT: Still, she's one of the few great Hollywood stars you never directed in a movie.

CUKOR: She was convinced she didn't play Scarlett O'Hara in *Gone with the Wind* because I favored Kate Hepburn.

LAMBERT: Back to Rochester. You were running this company in the summer and going back to New York in the winter?

CUKOR: Yes, and the second winter Frances Goldwyn introduced me to Gilbert Miller. He was looking for a young assistant and I got the job. This was in 1926. Gilbert Miller was a man of great taste and knowledge and he produced plays in both New York and London. I learned a lot from him, and I began directing for him. The first thing I did was Maugham's *The Constant Wife* with Ethel Barrymore. Then there was *Young Love* with Dorothy Gish, and two plays with Laurette Taylor, *Her Cardboard Lover* and *The Furies* by Zoë Akins.

LAMBERT: Years later, of course, you directed the movie of *Her Cardboard Lover*. But weren't there problems with the Laurette Taylor production?

CUKOR: Laurette was magic, it was comedy playing at its peak, it was brilliant—but it wasn't really right. She was in her early forties and too old for the part of this young woman frantically expecting her lover and undressing on the stage and all that kind of thing. After we'd played a few weeks out of town, Gilbert Miller closed the production. For New York he replaced Laurette with Jeanne Eagels, who wasn't a patch on her and whom I never got along with, anyway. Perhaps the play was most rightly cast when Tallulah did it in London.

LAMBERT: What about *The Furies*?

CUKOR: She had a great success in that.

LAMBERT: Was working with her your first experience of rapport with a great actress?

CUKOR: I think I had it from the start. And with actors as well. Later, in movies, I got tagged as a "woman's director," even though I used to point out (modestly, of course) that I'd worked rather well with Jack Barrymore, Spencer Tracy, Cary Grant, and so on. As far as I'm concerned, acting is acting, great acting is great acting, it excites me and I respond to it. As a movie director I began to flourish in the days of the great movie queens, and they were somehow more spectacular than the men, and I suppose this accounts for that label. In fact, I think actresses are tougher and more realistic than men. You can always talk turkey with them. For the three years I worked with Gilbert Miller I continued running the Rochester company in the summers, and through my new connections I persuaded various famous actresses to come down and do a play there—something that hadn't been heard of in forty years. Billie Burke, an enormous dramatic star at that time, came down, and Ruth Gordon, and Marjorie Rambeau. . . . Then the talkies came. Everything was split asunder and the world fell apart. There was a great demand in Hollywood for anyone who knew anything about the theater, who could help the actors speak the "titles," as they called dialogue at first. A whole bunch of us was transported to California. I went out under contract to Paramount, early in February, 1929. It's the only exact date I remember in my life.

Hollywood in 1929

LAMBERT: Did you take to films at once, or were you still snooty about them?

CUKOR: I was immediately fascinated, I liked the place and I was caught up in the whole thing.

LAMBERT: Katharine Hepburn says that, like a little boy, you still are.

CUKOR: But it wasn't easy for me at first. I'd learned a lot in the theater, I had the *métier*. Films were completely new, and everything about them had to be learned, too.

LAMBERT: Did you miss the theater at all?

CUKOR: No, I just took to the movies, I fell in love with the movies, Hollywood, everything! (And nowadays, unless the theater is absolutely first class, which it rarely is, I'm bored to death.) I arrived in Hollywood at a completely fascinating time, the climate was a mixture of confidence and chaos. The theater was going into one of its periodic low ebbs, the theater-going habit was dwindling, and road companies had almost disappeared. The movies had taken over both, just as television took over B movies many years later. And you couldn't make a failure in Hollywood

Grumpy, 1930, Cukor's first film as co-director: on location

in those days. The producing companies owned the movie theaters as well, people were hypnotized by sound, and any picture with sound would do business—rather like the nudies now. (Also, "simple" folk didn't need the Museum of Modern Art to tell them Chaplin was good, they just went to see the show.) Just before I left New York, I saw a picture called *In Old Arizona*, and there was a scene in which somebody fried eggs. The audience was thrilled by the sound of frying eggs! It was a total revolution, like color and the big screens later. Technically sound was still in a state of pandemonium. Most of the sound men were radio operators from boats; they'd never been anywhere near showbiz. You had to shoot at night because the stages weren't soundproofed. Everything that had been learned in silent pictures was abandoned, because the cameras weren't soundproofed either, and you couldn't move them. All that was soundproofed was three or four

John Barrymore takes a
break during *Romeo
and Juliet*

Fredric March does
John Barrymore in *The
Royal Family of
Broadway*

booths, with a camera placed in each. They had different lenses and shot the same scene simultaneously, like television later.

LAMBERT: What was your first assignment as dialogue director?

CUKOR: *River of Romance*, an adaptation of a charming play by Booth Tarkington called *Magnolia*. It was a quite brilliant, ironic story of the South. My main job was to coach the actors in a Southern accent. I could only do a very bogus one myself, but it seemed to work. One thing I noticed at once: the dialogue had a rather extraordinary quality, because many of those early Southern aristocrats were quite illiterate, and Tarkington reproduced this very well. However, it was lost on the producer and director. They'd look at some scene he'd written and say, "Well, it's entertainment only up to *here*," and cut the rest. The whole style of Booth Tarkington, his really marvelous quintessence of Southern speech, eluded them.

LAMBERT: What came next?

CUKOR: I met David Selznick, and we became great friends, and he recommended me to Lewis Milestone, who was about to make *All Quiet on the Western Front*. I shot all the tests for the actors—

LAMBERT: How much did you know about the camera then?

CUKOR: Nothing! I started from scratch, I watched and learned. (I seem to have done tests of everybody, by the way. They should put "He made an awful lot of tests" on my gravestone.) The vitality and strength of *All Quiet* is certainly Milestone's, but I also had a lot to do with directing the intimate scenes. Most of the actors then had no theater training, they didn't know what this peculiar thing called dialogue was. Without talk, they could behave in an effective way—but dialogue really threw them. Later, Janet Gaynor told me how in silent pictures they would only rehearse up to a certain point. Then the director would shoot the scene and talk all the way through it to the actors, giving them movements and so on. "Go on," he'd say. "The gate opens, you hear it, then you hear footsteps, then the doorbell. . . ." Curiously enough, these silent actors didn't look like puppets, they often had great individuality, even while they were playing this way.

LAMBERT: And yet very few of them made successful transitions from silent pictures to the talkies. Offhand, I can only think of Garbo, the Barrymores, Norma Shearer—

CUKOR: Yes, Norma Shearer went straight in, wonderfully guided by her husband, Irving Thalberg. Garbo's transition was very interesting. I remember her in her first sound picture, and her voice wasn't flexible at all. Although she'd had some theater training, she wasn't in command of it. Sometimes the gestures and movements were wonderful, but the voice—in *Romance*, for example—just couldn't match them. She spoke English with not the most distinguished accent, but she worked on it, and she has a very sensitive ear, and her speech became an individual speech. But you're right, very few of the great stars of the thirties had been in silent pictures, and very few of them had theater training. What they had was something quite different, "personality," that mysterious thing which touches the audience's imagination, and it could come from anywhere—a child like Shirley Temple or a vaudevillian like Mae West. Some of the most successful silent screen actors found themselves completely at a loss when they had to speak. I remember working with that wretched Adolphe Menjou. He was famous for doing a lot of polished, urbane business, and he didn't know how to integrate it with speaking. "My transitions," he used to complain, "oh, my *transitions!*"

LAMBERT: After your stint as dialogue director, you were signed by Paramount, I think, to co-direct some films—

CUKOR: Yes, I did three in a row, two of them with Cyril Gardner, a cutter and a very knowledgeable fellow. The first was *Grumpy*, from a very old-fashioned English play, with the English actor Cyril Maude. Then came *The Virtuous Sin*, which Louis Gasnier co-directed. It was from some Hungarian play, and it wasn't much good either. Happily, some prints of movies *have* been lost, and this was before the days of the archives, and I'd be in great shock if they rescued this one. (I remember that I enjoyed working with Kay Francis and Walter Huston, though.) And the third was *The Royal Family of Broadway*, from a play that was quite a hit at the time.

The Royal Family of Broadway
(1930)

CUKOR: This was the way Cyril Gardner and I worked together: I would stage the scenes, then he would photograph them. It was an extension of the way I worked with Milestone on *All Quiet*, except that now I was responsible for the actual staging of all the scenes.

LAMBERT: And Gardner made sure that everything would cut together?

CUKOR: Yes.

LAMBERT: The play itself is a kind of *You Can't Take It with You* about a family of actors.

CUKOR: But more pretentious. With something of the same tone, maybe—it was written by the same team, George Kaufman and Edna Ferber, who later did *Dinner at Eight*. The family was based on the Barrymores. Ethel Barrymore, who was already a friend of mine, was livid about the whole thing. She regarded anything written about the Barrymores as treason and invasion of privacy, but later she forgave everybody. I saw the picture again about ten years ago—there was some talk of doing a remake—and it struck me as very conventional in its ideas about the theater. At the time, however, it was a prestige success. Fredric March, who played John Barrymore, had actually met him and did a very clever impersonation. But the most interesting thing for me was working with Ina Claire, who played the actress based on Ethel.

LAMBERT: She's incredibly expert.

CUKOR: Her whole career was dedicated to perfecting herself. She started out as a mimic, then went into musical comedy and played the lead in *The Quaker Girl*. She sang and danced extremely well and became a big musical star. But she always held her head high and had a lot of class. Then she went into the Follies and did some brilliant satirical songs, and then David Belasco engaged her for a play called *Polly with a Past*. In that one she was a girl from Ohio who for plot reasons impersonated a

The Royal Family of Broadway: Ina Claire, Fredric March and Henrietta Crossman as the Barrymores

brilliant French actress. And then she learned that most difficult of arts, high comedy. Toward the end of her career, before she retired, she played in T. S. Eliot's *The Confidential Clerk*.

LAMBERT: She was superb as the grand duchess in the Garbo movie *Ninotchka*.

CUKOR: So elegant! A career of real artistic development.

LAMBERT: About *The Royal Family of Broadway* itself I have to agree with you. It's stagebound, and stagebound to a very dated play.

CUKOR: The smell of the greasepaint isn't real; it's plastic. But it represented what people at that time liked to believe about the theater.

LAMBERT: And as an early talkie it shows all the signs of that primitive television technique you were describing earlier.

CUKOR: Except, if I may say so, for one moment. You remember when Freddie March says, "Come on upstairs, everyone, while I take a bath"? Well, it occurred to me, Why don't we follow him all the way up that big staircase and take him to the bath? It was quite a business, because those huge cranes didn't operate electrically then as they do now—they were manually operated and very unwieldy. Still, we brought it off, we started on him downstairs, carried him and the whole family upstairs, then cut as he entered the bedroom and followed him to the shower. It was the beginning of a breakthrough for me, making the camera much more mobile.

Tarnished Lady
(1931)
Girls About Town
(1931)

LAMBERT: Your first picture as solo director, *Tarnished Lady*, is a much freer piece of work. You can tell it was written for the movies, not translated from the stage. It moves very naturally over a lot of New York locations, and the interior scenes are much less theatrical.

CUKOR: The script was written by Donald Ogden Stewart, with whom I worked later on *Holiday* and *The Philadelphia Story*. Yes, we certainly moved around a lot—along streets, in and out of churches. There was one scene shot on the actual terrace of a New York apartment.

LAMBERT: That must be when Clive Brook asks Tallulah Bankhead to marry him. I was struck by how real it looked—no taint of process work in that whole vista of New York beyond the terrace.

CUKOR: It seems to be a great recent discovery that you can actually shoot on location in New York. But they shot a lot of silent pictures there and we must have done half of *Tarnished*

Lady that way. (*A shrug*) I suppose the people who make such a critical fuss about all this never saw them.

LAMBERT: It was Tallulah Bankhead's first sound film. I imagine it was conceived as a vehicle for her?

CUKOR: Yes. The story was updated Edith Wharton, about a girl intent on keeping up her social position after her family loses its money. A very popular type of heroine at the time.

LAMBERT: It's strange how Bankhead doesn't really come off in the picture. She has some interesting moments, she surprises you from time to time, the personality is there—but she's not really at ease in front of the camera. As if she can't look it in the eye.

CUKOR: Tallulah was a most exciting, brilliant actress on the stage and in real life a highly entertaining, warmhearted, outrageous and charming creature. As a very young girl she became a big success in England, and Mrs. Patrick Campbell once said, "Watching Tallulah Bankhead on the stage is like watching somebody skating over very thin ice—and the English want to be there when she falls through." They were absolutely fascinated by her. But I don't think her quality of excitement ever quite worked on the screen. And she wanted to look like Garbo, that was her image of herself—high cheekbones and slightly tubercular hollow cheeks. (Later, the ladies wanted to look like gypsies, lots of hair and scarves and rings.) On the stage she had beautiful coloring, and on the screen she had beautiful bones, but her eyes were not eyes for movies. They looked somehow hooded and dead. And the face didn't move as well as the most successful faces do. Being photogenic is a question of movement, how the face moves. Her smile didn't illuminate, when she spoke her mouth didn't look graceful, and her eyes never really lighted up. Maybe if she'd started very, very young she might have developed into a real movie actress. But she had this great career on the stage, and movies were never easy for her, she wasn't born for them. She did more pictures later on, of course, and was diverting in them, though always slightly synthetic.

LAMBERT: In *Tarnished Lady* she's really miscast—some of the comedy scenes she does brilliantly, but when she has to be vulnerable and helpless, you just don't believe it.

CUKOR: And the climax of the story was so *silly!* She trusted this young man, she was in love with him, and just because she went to his apartment one day and found this adventuress talking

Tallulah in *Tarnished Lady*

LEFT: *Girls About Town*:
Kay Francis, Joel McCrea

RIGHT: *Girls About Town*:
Eugene Pallette, Lilyan
Tashman

to him—only *talking*, mind you—she was crushed. She never gave him a chance to explain, she just. . . . (*Amused*) But the audience of the time understood that. They enjoyed it, they liked seeing a woman crushed that way. Odd how that kind of convention looks absolutely incomprehensible thirty years later!

LAMBERT: *Girls About Town* is more hard-boiled and much more successful, I think—a romp in the early thirties "gold diggers" tradition.

CUKOR: It was written by Zoë Akins, a distinguished playwright, and she'd already done something else about tarts called *The Greeks Had a Word for It*. On the screen, because of censorship, there was a kind of innocence about her tarts. They had lovely clothes and lots of money and a succession of rich men who were mad about them, but they always said "Good night" at the door. Of course the audience smelled something, they thought, "Well, they may say 'good night,' but where the hell do they get all those clothes?" But, as you say, it was frankly a romp.

LAMBERT: Very lightly and deftly done. The acting is real movie acting, and Lilyan Tashman is brilliant, with something of a Harlow quality.

CUKOR: She was a great friend of mine and a very diverting creature. Before this, she'd played heavies. They never let her be as amusing on the screen as she was in real life. I was able to relax her, and that's why we got a good deal of her real personality, outrageous and cheerful and good-hearted. Very dashing and gotten up, too! How about Kay Francis? Wasn't she decorative?

LAMBERT: They make a good contrast. Tashman's so direct, and Kay Francis was always a bit schmaltzy—she wore clothes very well and managed to signal that her happiness wouldn't last, there'd be tears after the party. Almost like a silent movie heroine.

CUKOR: I liked their elegance. Lil had all that vigor and fun and I was glad I could bring it out. That's happened a few times in my career and it's always fascinated me.

LAMBERT: The other quality of the film is its sheer professionalism. You tell the story so well on its own flimsy terms. The comedy is very sharply paced, and I particularly liked the scene where the two girls decide to raise money by auctioning off all their clothes. It turns into a very rowdy situation of elegant whores selling their ill-gotten gains to their elegant whore friends. The tone of it looks ahead to *The Women*.

CUKOR (*surprised*): I don't remember that too well. I chiefly remember how charming the girls were, and Joel McCrea being very attractive as the young man. Also a funny old character boy called Eugene Pallette.

LAMBERT: There's one location scene which is the kind of thing your later movies specialize in. It's quite elaborately staged, yet unobtrusive at the same time. Kay Francis and Joel McCrea go to the zoo, and the camera follows them with a long dolly shot as they walk past the various cages, interrupting their dialogue from time to time to look at the animals.

CUKOR: You know, I don't remember that well either! It's funny how standards change. *The Royal Family* had much more "prestige" at the time, and this one seemed just an amusing, routine picture. But from what you say I'm sure *Girls About Town* holds up much better.

LAMBERT: It's a real movie.

CUKOR: And people go for that these days.

LAMBERT: I suppose the fashionable attitude to movies at that time is summed up in one line from *The Royal Family*—and it does come out funny. Ina Claire and her actress mother are riding home in a cab from the theater. They pass through Times Square and the old lady glances out the window at a movie marquee. She comments, "All singing, all dancing, all terrible!"

CUKOR: Yes, that was exactly the fashionable attitude.

Interlude:
On Trouble in Paramount

LAMBERT: We now come to what must have been a very unhappy experience, when you were assigned to direct *One Hour with You.*

CUKOR: By this time Paramount apparently thought I was quite promising. Lubitsch had already done a couple of very successful pictures with Chevalier and Jeannette MacDonald and had already written the script for this one. But he was busy on another picture, an antiwar thing called *The Man I Killed,* so I was asked to direct it instead. With the best intentions in the world, I couldn't do a Lubitsch picture. Lubitsch was what they really wanted and what they should have had.

LAMBERT: How long were you actually on the picture?

CUKOR: I directed for about two weeks. I didn't like Chevalier, and he didn't like me, but Jeannette MacDonald and I subsequently became very good friends, and she wanted me to do a picture with her. We shot an English and a French version simultaneously. Then B. P. Schulberg, the head of the studio, saw a lot of rushes and didn't like them. Lubitsch had now finished shooting *The Man I Killed,* but they didn't officially "remove" me. What happened was goddamned agony for me. I was under contract and had to stay on the picture, on the set, while Lubitsch took over.

LAMBERT: Why was this?

CUKOR: Well, Lubitsch still couldn't give a hundred percent of his time to it, because he was cutting the other picture and so on. I still did a few things, I carried them out the way he wanted, but for most of the time I just sat there and really did less than when I was a dialogue director. I behaved very well, I think. I was very disciplined and acted as if I didn't mind. Officially I finished the picture, but Lubitsch really directed it.

LAMBERT: Did he reshoot what you'd already done?

CUKOR: No. I admire Lubitsch very much, but he shot things in a highly stylized way that is simply not my own. And we had a different approach to language. Lubitsch never really spoke English very well, and it didn't finally matter in his case, but it led him to do things I couldn't do. For instance, he'd cast a very Middle Western actor like George Barbier to play the Emperor Franz Joseph. This is something he'd never have permitted in German, where he was sensitive to the nuances of speech. There was a very pretty German actress called Camilla Horn, and they cast her in some classical German part, and Lubitsch was very amused because she spoke what he called drugstore German.

LAMBERT: That's interesting, because I always thought Lubitsch's casting of rather crude middle-class actors to play aristocrats and emperors was a piece of calculated satire, a sort of deliberate effrontery.

CUKOR: There's a way of making an emperor middle-class and rather bourgeois, and you still believe him as an emperor. I don't think Lubitsch was aware of that. It was still funny, the way Lubitsch did it, but I don't believe it was funny in the way he intended. Anyway, after I'd sat on the set and watched Lubitsch direct, and minded my p's and q's, Mr. Schulberg called me into his office. "I'm going to ask you to do me a little favor," he said. Mind you, he was all-powerful, and I was less than the dust beneath his chariot wheels. "I'd like you to take your name off the picture," he said. And I refused. If he didn't want my name on the picture, he should have taken me off after the first two weeks. "Well," Mr. Schulberg said, "I'm taking your name off, anyway."

I told him I'd sue, and I did. I wanted to leave the studio anyway, David Selznick had gone over to RKO and wanted me to work for him there. Out of sheer devilry, and because he didn't like Selznick, Schulberg wouldn't let me go. It was the only time I came face-to-face with this kind of politicking. But I went ahead and sued Paramount, and it was settled out of court. Part of the settlement was that they canceled my contract and allowed me to go to RKO. For some time there was a coolness between myself and Lubitsch. He probably thought I wanted to take credit for something I didn't do. But I don't believe anyone should be cheated out of a credit when it matters; I've always made a great point of that for myself and other people.

LAMBERT: Did your Paramount contract still have a while to run?

CUKOR: Yes. Not that it mattered. I wasn't getting all that much money. And RKO took over the contract, so I didn't get a rise in salary. Later the same thing happened when Metro took over my RKO contract. But the important thing was, I got to work with David on his first picture at RKO, *What Price Hollywood?*

What Price Hollywood?
(1932)
A Star Is Born
(1954)

L AMBERT: Of your two movies about Hollywood, *What Price Hollywood?* strikes me as done very skillfully from the outside, but *A Star Is Born* is in every sense an inside job. I know we're talking about an early and a later work, and in the years between your own experience of Hollywood must have grown much richer. But the *What Price Hollywood?* script is only so-so, and it needed an exciting actress to lift it up. I don't find Constance Bennett that kind of actress.

CUKOR: And yet, to an audience at that time, she *was*. Dorothy Parker wrote a wonderful preface to James Thurber's first collection of drawings, *The Seal in the Bedroom*—just turn off your machine until I find that book. . . .

(He goes to the library and returns with the book)

Now. . . . *(Reads)* "These are strange people that Mr. Thurber has turned loose upon us. . . . The women are of a dowdiness so overwhelming that it becomes tremendous style. Once a heckler, who should have been immediately put out, complained that the Thurber women had no sex appeal. The artist was no more than reproachful. 'They have for my men,' he said." (*Closes book*) That's what I mean about Connie Bennett. In those days she was on the crest of the wave and supplied something an audience found glamorous. And the whole enterprise was very dear to David Selznick's heart. He later used the same story in a different way for the first version of *A Star Is Born*, with Janet Gaynor and Fredric March. Like the audience at that time, Selznick had a very romantic view of Hollywood, a real love of it. (The talkies started out being fascinated by the theater, and then it became the other way around. For better or worse, movies have great prestige and influence now, and the theater hardly exists.) Largely through David's influence, we didn't kid the basic idea of Hollywood. Most of the other Hollywood pictures make it a kind of crazy, kooky place, but to David it was absolutely real, he believed in it. I think that's why *What Price Hollywood?* was one of the few successful pictures about the place, in the face of a tradition that they never succeed. Of course, all these superstitions and ideas of "good taste" become absurd in fifty years, but I'm telling you this to explain how David's idea of Hollywood coincided with people's built-in romantic aspirations about it.

LAMBERT: The connection between these two pictures is obvious, of course—the star on the way up contrasted with the director or actor on the way down, and the idea that, in spite of personal heartbreak, the show must go on.

CUKOR: And not done cynically. After all, it's something that happens.

LAMBERT: The incidental details in *What Price Hollywood?* are very convincing—that scene of Constance Bennett rehearsing by herself, over and over again, the little bit she's been given in her first picture. It's just a tiny scene coming down a staircase, with a throwaway line, but she's so nervous and bad when they shoot it, the director fires her. She goes home and stays up all night trying to make it better. You see her gradually improving, regaining her nerve, and in the end she does it quite decently. Then she calls up the director, Lowell Sherman, and says, "Give me another chance." He does, of course, and she's very good, and this moment turns her into a star because the producer sees the dailies and puts her under contract. A very tricky thing to make believable, even though it can happen. But you make it believa-

What Price Hollywood? Aspiring actress (Constance Bennett, center)
and director (Lowell Sherman)

ble by showing the reality to her ambition and the dogged way
she works at it.

Cukor: Yes, the way she just goes over and over the scene,
without an intellectualizing drama coach or crap like that. But
didn't you find Lowell Sherman brilliant as the director? He was
a very fine actor, but there was something about him, a slightly
odious quality, that kept him from being a real star. It worked
very well in this story.

Lambert: Yes, you felt his drunkenness and disagreeable behavior came out of a bitterness and a feeling he was a basically
unattractive person. He made you believe he was a talented director, too.

Cukor: Which made his suicide touching.

[47]

LAMBERT: There's an interesting effect in that scene. I don't know who created it—there's credit for "special effects" to Slavko Vorkapich—but just before he shoots himself you have a series of flash cutaways, very quick shots, in which he and the audience relive his life. You see him in his early triumphant days, then progressively more haggard and desperate.

CUKOR: I don't remember that. But I do remember an extraordinary sound effect when you felt his brain was bursting. That was done in the simplest way. Somebody in the sound department took a cigar box, tied it by a string from the inside and wheeled it around. It created this whirring sound, a sound of turmoil. . . . What about the comedy? Is it still funny—the rather daffy love scenes between Connie Bennett and the polo player?

LAMBERT: They don't really hold up, I'm afraid. But I liked another comedy scene, when the gossip columnist interviews the star about her love life. That's very sharp.

CUKOR: And the script conference scene, when the Negro maid, Louise Beavers, makes an idiotic suggestion and they throw her in the pool? (*Amused*) There'd be a great outcry if we did that now. . . . Well, it was a mixed bag. Some of it funny and bright. And a big success at the time.

LAMBERT: For *A Star Is Born* you had a far superior script and, even more important, a wonderful actress at the center. The situations are very similar, but with Judy Garland your star becomes a tragic and complex figure.

CUKOR: Yes, but it's one of the sad things of all time, the way the studio cut that picture! They not only cut it, they took the negative away and melted it down for silver. Judy Garland and I felt like the English queen who had "Calais" engraved on her heart. Bloody Mary, wasn't it? Neither of us could ever bear to see the final version.

LAMBERT: What were the main cuts? I know the "Born in a Trunk" number was added later. Who directed that, by the way?

CUKOR: The man who did the choreography. I don't remember his name.* Gene Allen and George Hoyningen-Huene helped on it, and also Roger Edens, who was a specialist in musical numbers. . . . But they cut so many important scenes. The romance between Judy Garland and James Mason was much more clearly developed. There was an excellent scene when they quarrel and

* Richard Barstow.

she runs away, and he tries to find her. He finally tracks her down to one of those terrible Los Angeles apartment buildings—she's on the roof, drying her hair, very embarrassed at being found there, and there's a rather spectacular vista of the whole city from this ugly, dreary roof. Then they go to a preview together, a charming scene when she's so nervous that she runs out, says, "Pardon me," and throws up near one of the big downtown oil pumps. And when he proposes to her, there's a wonderful number with both of them on a sound stage, she's recording a song, and there's an open microphone and everyone around can hear him proposing. . . .

LAMBERT: Did they make all these cuts because they thought the picture too long?

CUKOR: Yes, but it was ridiculous, because they also wanted to put more numbers in. When they added "Born in a Trunk," they made the picture twenty minutes longer. I knew it was too long, but I told them that Moss Hart and I—he wrote the script, you know, a really brilliant script—we could sweat out this twenty minutes and they'd never miss them. They refused, just went ahead with these lethal cuts and threw all the material away.

LAMBERT: In this case, who exactly were *they*?

CUKOR: I made the picture for Warner Brothers. But in the end *they* are always the same people.

LAMBERT: There's a rumor that someone, somehow, got hold of a complete sixteen-millimeter print, and it still exists.

CUKOR: I wish to Christ it could be shown.

LAMBERT: The picture's full of scenes with a very carefully rehearsed effect of spontaneity. A marvelous one is when Judy Garland tells Mason about the number she did at the studio that day—"Somewhere There's a Someone"—and makes fun of it.

CUKOR: Yes, a tour de force, but there was another even more effective one that they cut. Right after that agonizing scene in her dressing room, after Mason's death, she goes straight out and, in one shot, does a very cheerful number on the sound stage. It was wonderful the way she went straight into it.

LAMBERT: All these cuts explain the final effect of *A Star Is Born*. So many intriguing scenes, so many brilliant moments, but you come away with a fragmented feeling. It doesn't quite add up.

[49]

A Star Is Born: Judy
Garland as Esther
Blodgett

A Star Is Born: Judy
Garland as Vicki Lester

James Mason, Judy Garland in
A Star Is Born

A Star Is Born, one of the
scenes that was cut: Norman
Maine (James Mason) making
one of his swashbuckling
successes

CUKOR: The picture is totally fragmented. I think it accounts for why Judy Garland didn't win an Academy Award.

LAMBERT: Even with what's left, she should have won it. I wonder who got it that year. . . .*

CUKOR: She'd never played a serious part before this, she told me she'd never wept before on the screen, never screamed, never had a big scene.

LAMBERT: And James Mason, in his very tactful way, is just as remarkable.

CUKOR: It's just too bad the goddamned thing couldn't have been kept the way it was, long as it was.

LAMBERT: How did you feel about using CinemaScope? You dealt with that awful shape in a very skillful way—the idea of leaving both sides of the frame almost dark in several scenes—

CUKOR: There were a lot of technical difficulties because they weren't sure about the lenses then, and unless the exposure was absolutely right, everything would turn red. You were supposed to play everything on a level plane, with no depth of focus. There was almost no movement up and down, back and away from the camera. And you weren't supposed to come in really close on faces. Almost everything, apparently, had to be thrown away. Well, we shot like that for one day—and then, with Gene Allen and George Huene, we said, "To hell with it." We just paid no attention to that unfortunate mailbox shape, we ignored all the rules, we even cut much more quickly than we were supposed to. It was rather like what happened when sound came in, you were told to abandon everything you'd learned.

LAMBERT: The very quick cutting is extremely effective at the scene of the premiere, with the hysteria and surging crowds and photographers' flashbulbs—

CUKOR: You know, I'm amused at so many "discoveries." A great deal of that was shot with a hand-held camera, which became the latest thing a few years later.

LAMBERT: A lot of people have commented on one very striking image before James Mason walks into the ocean. He's in the beach house, surrounded by windows and sliding glass doors. He stands on one side of the screen, reflected in a window, and on the other side you see a big panorama of the ocean—

CUKOR (*amused*): But there wasn't a beach house! There was

* Grace Kelly, for *The Country Girl*.

[52]

an interior set, and we had to suggest the location by a process shot of the reflection of the ocean.

LAMBERT: So it was one of those very successful things dictated by necessity?

CUKOR: Oh, yes, all we had was the interior set and a little exterior set of the terrace right outside the house. But we kept the exterior alive, there was a sense of movement in the air. Judy Garland wore a very light chiffon scarf, and the air moved it. It was tricky, because if we'd had a regular fan, we'd have had to postsync the dialogue. So we made wind tunnels, where the fan is placed outside the studio and the air brought in through a big canvas tunnel that kills the sound. So you got the illusion of being at the ocean. I don't like doing exteriors on an interior set, but if you keep the air going you can keep the scene alive.

LAMBERT: We could talk about several more scenes, because the texture of the picture is so subtle. But I'd like to ask you about the one where the agent goes to visit Mason in the sanitarium. It has such a strange and chilling atmosphere.

CUKOR: I'll tell you where I got that from. Years ago, when I was going to direct *Camille*, I went to see Jack Barrymore about playing De Varville, the part Henry Daniell finally played. Jack had put himself into some kind of home in Culver City to stop drinking. He was a friend of mine, and I went to take the script to him. It was an old frame house that called itself a rest home. I went into some dreary, depressing room. Back of it was the dining room, and I noticed something that always strikes me as very shabby and sad. They hadn't taken away the tablecloths, and you knew they never changed them. Then Jack came in, with a sort of aide called Kelly. He took us into a gloomy sitting room and said, "Can we sit in here, Kelly? Nobody's going to come through and disturb us by pretending he's Napoleon." I reported this episode to David Selznick, who was preparing the first *A Star Is Born* with William Wellman. They liked the scene so much they included it in the picture. Then, years later, I found myself redoing it.

Interlude:
On the Climate on the Set

CUKOR: The climate on the set includes relations with the actors, and with everybody, in fact. The hours are very long. You've got to be perfectly natural about the whole thing. No patronizing, no putting on airs. You're spoiled when you're on the set, because you're the master. You're physically spoiled—you're in the depths of the desert and you say, "I want a Coca-Cola," and this wonderful property man brings it to you. I'm talking now, I suppose, about the "old world" crews, the crews that have been part of a tradition of moviemaking here since 1910. . . . Anyway, the password to everything, at least for me, is a kind of humor. You're on the set under great strain from eight in the morning until seven at night, there are moments when you're desperately serious, but you can't spend that long day with a cathedral hush over the whole place. I like the set to be lively. I don't mind noise, and things like that. But then I get very testy. I've got sharp ears and I'm very curious. If there's a whisper on the set, I'm very curious to know what it is, even though it throws me. I like everybody to be working in a perfectly relaxed manner. I enjoy just talking. I don't mind listening to lousy jokes. Sometimes people are surprised because all this looks rather permissive. But there is great discipline behind it all. When it's supposed to be quiet, it really is quiet. That's a wonderful thing about a movie set. At one moment it seems pandemonium, then suddenly everybody is doing his job, doing it very well, and it all falls into place. People know where they're supposed to be, what they're supposed to do. The only time they get slapped down is if they violate that rule. One thing that drives me absolutely up the wall is when visitors come on the set and show bad manners by gawking and getting in the eyeline of the actors. I make everyone shoo them away.

LAMBERT: That's your threshold of pain?

CUKOR: Yes—but let me tell you how *I* violate other people's threshold of pain. While I'm watching the scene being shot, I'm quite unaware that I make a lot of grotesque faces. Some of the pictures taken of me on the set are absolutely grotesque! During *The Women* I found that Rosalind Russell, who has beautiful manners, was constantly breaking up. Finally I said, "Christ, the scene's not *that* funny, why are you laughing so much?" "It's you," she said. "I look out and see you going through all those emotions." So I said, "That's all right. What the hell, I'm glad you told me," and went and hid behind the camera and continued making those faces. Actresses particularly have sharp ears and eyes and sensibilities, and dolphins have got nothing on them for personal radar. Once I did a scene with Joan Crawford when she had her back to the camera. At the end she said, "You didn't like it." I asked how she knew. "I saw you looking interested up to a certain point," she said, "and then you went *Ugh!*" But she'd never looked in my direction at all.

LAMBERT: Visible or not, you're the audience.

CUKOR: Yes, the director is also the audience, a discriminating audience that is to be trusted. I trust any audience in a way, just because it's *there*. I'm very aware of this when I see someone else's picture at a preview, and I can feel where a scene works up to a certain point, then it goes off. Very often you can't see that with your own pictures, even though you're watching every frame. But when you're watching something with an audience, you may be offended by their reaction, but it's *there* and it makes you aware of something you hadn't noticed before.

[55]

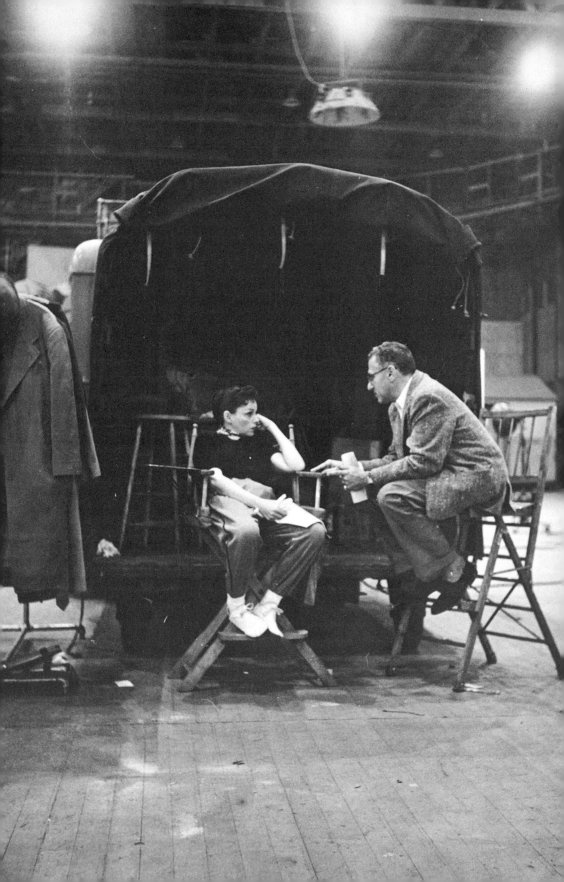

Directing the masked ball in *Justine*

LAMBERT: As an audience of one, when you're directing, how do you react?

CUKOR: My first reaction is always emotional. Even when I describe scenes, I describe them emotionally. I don't weep or anything, but there's always some part of me left bloody on the scene I've just directed. That's what gives it intensity. Then there are technical things—I may change the lighting or tell an actor, "You were slow on that"—but it's always the emotional impact first. Also, a director has to be able to solve certain things, to see what's wrong. He has to be constantly improving, refining, and to do this properly he has to know the people with whom he's working. Some people require a very light and careful touch, others

The climate on the set: with Judy Garland during *A Star Is Born* need coaching. You've got to learn what throws them off, and you've got to know the actor so well that you can judge exactly how it's going to look on the screen. Sometimes you're surprised, sometimes you're fooled. You can't always know exactly what you're going to get, but that, as they say, is showbiz.

LAMBERT: How do you try to get what you hope to get?

CUKOR: By pressing different buttons. Above all, you've got to be *on the level.* There must be no bullshit from you or anyone else. And people mustn't have reservations, they mustn't say "Yes, yes" and then pull their punches. Same with me to them. One thing that makes me absolutely ruthless is when I feel a person is saying "Yes" to me but really thinking he's going to get away with something else. To spot when it's faked and when it's good your senses must be constantly alert. You've got to have complete faith in your own reactions, for better or for worse, so that you can make snap judgments, then and there. One thing I seldom do is look through the camera. I always have to remind myself to check things first through the camera, because I prefer to watch the scene itself with my own eyes. I feel I don't lose any human contact that way. Once again, this is a question of letting nothing get in the way of a direct emotional reaction. In the same way, I react emotionally to the rushes and the rough cut. Later, it filters through my mind. Finally, when I feel I've done all I can, I withdraw and leave it on the lap of the gods, the audience. Another important thing—when I'm working, I always think, "Don't dilute it." You make a little compromise here, another one there, and it's diluted.

LAMBERT: The kind of dilution that might occur as the result of working under pressure?

CUKOR: Yes, settling for the costume that isn't quite right or the scene that seems to lack something. I admire people who are absolutely stubborn and immovable. I'm not always stubborn enough, which is wrong. Things have to come out with their absolute full force. I feel that very, very much.

A Bill of Divorcement
(1932)
Dinner at Eight
(1933)

LAMBERT: Clemence Dane's play *A Bill of Divorcement* looks pretty dated now. But seeing the film again, two things about it were still very interesting. It's your first picture with Katharine Hepburn—

CUKOR: Her first picture, too.

LAMBERT: Yes. And she's so striking and original, so completely *there* already. One senses how well you worked together from the start. And then there's a short sequence in this early picture that seems to me to contain the essence of your style.

CUKOR *(surprised)*: In this picture? Really?

LAMBERT: It lasts only a couple of minutes and has no dialogue. John Barrymore has escaped from the asylum and returned home. His daughter, played by Hepburn, is alone in the house when he arrives. She hides halfway up the stairs and watches him wander around the room, looking at photographs, noticing things that have changed. . . . It's a very kinetic little scene, with a beautiful tension.

CUKOR: I can tell you about that. The scene is a situation when all the daughter knows about her father is that he was shell-shocked during the war. She never knew him; it's not very real to her. Now the father comes back. What makes the situation touching is that *we* know—but *he* doesn't—that his wife is in love with someone else and wants to get rid of him. I'd never worked with Jack Barrymore before, but I found him very accessible from the beginning. When he did the scene the first time, it had the wrong kind of tension. It was too desperate. I said, "Jack, the man is happy to be home, he doesn't know they don't want him." He understood this at once and played it the way you see, and that's what made it poignant. About Kate—she and two other girls were up for the part. With David Selznick, who produced the picture, I saw a test that she'd done in New York. She was quite unlike anybody I'd ever seen. Though she'd never made a movie, she had this very definite knowledge and feeling right from the start.

A Bill of Divorcement: Katharine Hepburn in her first film, with
Henry Stephenson and John Barrymore

Marie Dressler in *Dinner at Eight*

Jean Harlow and Wallace Beery in *Dinner at Eight*. "The same situation was done supremely well in *Born Yesterday*"

LAMBERT: Almost forty years later she comes across as so contemporary. It's not only the part—being against her family, against middle-class values, and so on—but you sense that she's a natural rebel. She has an impatience and directness that must have been electric at the time.

CUKOR: Yes, that quality of cutting through "correctness." In that same scene we were talking about she did something fascinating. Her attitude was, "I never knew my father, how can I necessarily be expected to love him?" She hadn't the experience of an audience liking her on the screen yet, so she wasn't careful or cagey. A known and loved actress might do the scene very well, but in some way she'd indicate, "Of course, I'd never *really* be mean to my own father."

LAMBERT: Apart from Hepburn, the material dates because it's so wedded to British upper-middle-class attitudes of the period—all that graciousness. But I suppose when you were making it those attitudes seemed real and even admirable?

CUKOR: Yes, they seemed real. Although I think we glamorized them slightly. When I saw the picture again recently, I was very taken aback a few times. Kate has just been told there's a streak of insanity in the family, and the "wise" lawyer says, "Don't worry, everything will be all right." (*A grimace*) You know damn well it *won't* be all right! But this was a product of its period, well conceived but so romantically written it can embarrass you now. And then, putting in that scene at the end, that the father's musical gifts are coming back and he's going to write the great sonata—

LAMBERT: And the trashy music he starts playing. . . . That scene wasn't in the play?

CUKOR: Oh, dear, no, I'm afraid they invented it for the picture.

LAMBERT: *Dinner at Eight* is just as much of its period—but the period works positively for it. There's an underlying sense of the Depression behind all the comedy. It has an edge.

CUKOR: You felt that?

LAMBERT: That and the bitterness of all the characters. Everybody really hates everybody. Husbands cheat on wives, millionaires are scared of going broke—there's this constant suggestion of insecurity below the surface.

CUKOR: And the whole thing revolves around this dinner party given by a woman who is just a foolish snob. Yes, George Kaufman was quite an astringent writer, not very profound, but with the saving grace of being funny. The picture was very well cast, too, and I did it in twenty-seven or twenty-eight days. It's haunted me my entire career. People say, "Well, if you could do *that* one so quickly. . . ." I suppose it all went smoothly and well because of all those very expert actors. And there were no serious sustained scenes. It was my first encounter with Jean Harlow. I'd seen her in *Public Enemy* and *Hell's Angels*, where she was so bad and self-conscious it was comic. She got big laughs when she didn't want them. Then I saw *Red Dust*—and there she was, suddenly marvelous in comedy. A tough girl and yet very feminine, like Mae West. They both wisecrack, but they have something vulnerable, and it makes them attractive. Jean Harlow was very soft about her toughness. I liked that scene when she told off Wallace Beery. She's lying in bed, wearing a new hat—a black hat in an all-white bedroom. It was the first of those things, by the way—

LAMBERT: The first use of black and white in a stylized way?

CUKOR: Yes, the whole room is completely white. Then she puts on this black hat. They copied it subsequently a great deal. And when Wally Beery comes in, she sits up and pushes back her hat, as if she's sitting on the toilet. And she says, "You big windbag!" and so on, and doesn't pull her punches—she has such charm! And I'll never forget—when Wally Beery, who's a big businessman and kind of in with the government, says he has to go to Washington—I'll never forget the way she looks at him and says, "Yeah, you better go and fix things." (*Highly amused*) Like a waitress! Totally vague, no idea what it's really about!

LAMBERT: It sums up their marriage. She dislikes him but she thinks he's important.

CUKOR: And all his activities bore her. The same situation was done supremely well in *Born Yesterday*.

LAMBERT: I also like Barrymore very much in the film. He's always seemed to me at his best in comedy.

CUKOR: Although Jack was playing a second-rate actor, he had no vanity as such. He even put things in to make himself hammier, more ignorant. When they come to see him about a comeback and mention Ibsen, he had this wonderful idea. He said, "Ah, Ibsen!" and got up and leaned against the mantel and declaimed a bit of Oswald in *Ghosts*, getting it all wrong. "Oh,

Twilight of a star: John Barrymore in *Dinner at Eight*

"When I worked with the Barrymores, the residue remained of having
first seen them from the second balcony." With
John Barrymore on the set of *Dinner at Eight*

mother, forgive me . . . the sun. . . ." Then at the end, when he's
decided to kill himself, we thought that although he wanted to
die in a picturesque way, he should fuck that up, too. There was a
stool in the room, and I suggested he trip over it on his way to
take up a suitable pose. So he walked very grandly across the
room, then tripped, did this awful middle-aged sprawl, got up,
pulled himself together, sat down in a chair and turned his profile
to the light. . . . I've always found that if first-rate actors respect
you, they'll try anything.

LAMBERT: The third outstanding performance is by Marie
Dressler.

CUKOR: She was the biggest star of her time, you know, a sort of
low comedian and hokey-pokey, too. She ruled in musical comedy
and in low comedy. As time went on she acquired a kind of

peculiar distinction, a magnificence. She was a law unto herself. She'd mug and carry on—which she did in this picture—but she knew how to make an entrance with great aplomb, great effect. Of course, I couldn't really believe her as an ex-beauty, with all those lovers.

LAMBERT: Somehow it doesn't matter. She plays as if she knows it's all a joke. . . . Another point—both *A Bill of Divorcement* and *Dinner at Eight* are fairly early talkies, and both are adaptations of plays. It's the material that makes one of them fall down and the other stand up. The skill in both pictures is very equal, very unobtrusive—no attempt to do anything more than a straightforward filmed play. For instance, neither film contains a single exterior shot. Was that a conscious decision?

CUKOR: I don't remember.

LAMBERT: I wondered. . . . Years later, when Cocteau filmed his play *Les Parents Terribles*, the critics made a great point that there were no exteriors, and it was hailed as an experiment. But by the time you'd got as far in your career as *Dinner at Eight* how did you feel about directing movies? Obviously you were very interested in the work with actors, in getting movie performances. What else?

CUKOR: I'd begun knowing my way around. Cutting and things like that. The kind of acting that worked in pictures.

Interlude:
On Working with Actors

LAMBERT: You once said you don't like to talk the part too much with actors because you lose the magic.

CUKOR: I know I said that, but I still talk my head off. But I talk in a special way, I think, an immediate way. When I read what people are supposed to tell actors, it seems much too theoretical. You have to create your own language and your own image of whatever you're doing. On *A Woman's Face* I had an image for Joan Crawford's character for the first part of the picture, when her face is scarred. It was *mentalité du bossu*. If I felt she was forgetting this during a scene, I'd do a *mentalité du bossu* number at her from near the camera. (*Cukor twists his head to one side and makes a face like the Hunchback of Notre Dame.*) She'd see it and understand. On the first day of shooting *Gaslight* with Ingrid Bergman I wanted to try and keep up the intensity between takes, so I'd retell her the story, the emotional point the scene was leading up to. Finally she looked at me very politely and said, "I'm not a dumb Swede, you've told me that before." So I apologized and stopped, and then I got a little afraid of telling her other things. The result

[67]

was, after two or three more days the producer said, "These people are acting as though they're under water." I knew this was true, so I started talking to Ingrid just the way I'd done before, keeping up the pitch, retelling everything, and after a while she began to like it. It worked. But, of course, you always communicate with everyone in a different way, and you have to make it fresh every time.

LAMBERT: That must be based on your intuition about the people you're working with.

CUKOR: Intuition plus experience. When you finally get to know the person, you know what works. I never rehearse the emotions of a scene, by the way, only the mechanics. Garbo always worked that way, and wise movie people know about that, they go through the mechanics and then let it happen when the camera's turning. I used to urge Rex Harrison during *My Fair Lady*, "Don't play it, don't play it, let it come out later!" He had a tendency to give too much of himself in rehearsals. He's a most accomplished actor, and he knows that *you* know when it's right, so you don't tell someone like that how to read a line, you make a climate in which he can work and find things out for himself. Then you say, "That's it, you've got it." For different reasons it was the same thing with James Mason in *A Star Is Born*. James is a highly talented man but a reserved, rather enigmatic person, and I knew that his last scene in the picture, when he breaks down and decides to commit suicide, would be a case of letting him find things out for himself. So I let the camera stay on him for a very long time, and all his feelings came out and he became so involved, in fact, he could hardly stop.

LAMBERT: One of the reasons that Judy Garland's performance in that picture is so memorable is that you feel she, too, is discovering things for herself, and the emotion seems deeply personal.

CUKOR: Until *A Star Is Born* Judy Garland had only played musical comedy. A lot of people in musical comedy are like mimics or impersonators, which is not real acting. They promise more than they deliver. You think, "If only they could play out a scene, how good they'd be," and very often you're wrong. But Judy Garland was a very original and resourceful actress. Toward the end of shooting we had to do a scene when she's in a state of total depression after her husband's suicide. While we lined it up she just sat there, very preoccupied. We'd talked about the scene only a little, but we both had a general idea of what it should be.

Working with actors: with Fredric March on *Susan and God*

The basic note was her melancholia, her state of total depression. Just before the take I said to her very quietly, "You know what this is about. You really know this." She gave me a look, and I knew she was thinking, "He wants me to dig into myself because I know all about this in my own life." That was all. We did a take. If you remember the scene, she has trouble in articulating anything, she seems exhausted and dead. A friend, played by Tommy Noonan, comes to see her to try and persuade her to go to a benefit performance that night. He chides her about not giving in to herself, he even gets deliberately rough with her—and she loses her head. She gets up and screams like someone out of control, maniacal and terrifying. And when Judy Garland did this, it was *absolutely* terrifying! She had no concern with what she looked like, she went much further than I'd expected, and I thought it was great. But I was also scared that the actor might be thrown because of this tremendous impact on him. Not at all, he stayed right with her, at one moment he even grabbed her and she tried to get away. (You have to be careful about moments like that, they mustn't be too rehearsed or slick, and they mustn't be too goddamned much. But this was exactly right, an ugly, awkward, desperate scuffle.) So he grabbed her and held her and spoke his next lines with great force and energy. The lines were meant to shame her—and her reaction was unforgettable. She turned around, and you saw that all the anger and madness and fear had disappeared. Her face looked very vulnerable and tender, there were tears in her eyes. So I said, "Cut!" and then, "Quick, let's do it once more!" and they dried Judy off to get her ready again. One of the hazards of picture making, you see, is that you get a scene which turns out wonderfully, but next morning they tell you the sound was no good or there was a scratch on the film. That's why I wanted to do it again immediately. So Judy did it again—differently, but just as stunningly. Scenes can never be reproduced exactly, and you shouldn't try. (Our first take was technically okay, by the way.) Anyway, when it was over, I said to Judy, "You really scared the hell out of me." She was very pleased, she didn't realize what an effect she'd made. And then— she was always funny, she had this great humor—she said, "Oh, that's nothing. Come over to my house any afternoon. I do it every afternoon." Then she gave me a look and added, "But I only do it *once* at home."

LAMBERT: You said earlier that it's important to spot it immediately when an actor's faking. What are the signs of that?

CUKOR: Very often an actor does a scene and I say, "You think you're thinking, and you go through the mechanics of thinking— but you *aren't*, in fact, thinking." In the same way, an actor can make a big show of "sincerity." But you know when it's hokey-pokey because you see it *right up close*. That's the whole key to it. They discovered about *right up close* in the silent days, they broke away entirely from stage tradition for acting at close range. That's why there was no bullshit in the silent days. They had no words, just faces at close range, and they couldn't bluff. We've lost some of that today, especially in those movies with lots of fashionable cutting and effects and people flinging themselves around and suffering rather pretentiously. Maybe it fools a lot of people, but it doesn't fool me. Really sincere acting with very few tricks, someone like Gary Cooper, is dismissed with "Oh, but he's such a simple person, what he's playing is so simple." Look at it right up close. It's much more than that.

LAMBERT: And the best movie acting, someone like Gary Cooper, always *looks* spontaneous.

CUKOR: Particularly comedy. When I saw Ruth Gordon on the stage in *The Matchmaker*, a very good comedy performance, you could hardly believe she wasn't making everything up as it went along. One night I went backstage and saw her rehearsing every line before she went on to make it fresh. Improvisation can't achieve this—it can give you a couple of unexpectedly funny lines or moments, but that's all. Spencer Tracy had the gift of improvising occasionally *within* the scene. In *Adam's Rib* there was this moment when Kate Hepburn had bought a new hat—it looked chic but a little funny. Spence suddenly put in, "You look like Grandma Moses," very throwaway, and we kept it, because it came out of the scene and the moment. But then Spence, like all great comedy players, was humanly involved in what he was doing. It was the same thing with Judy Holliday. And even in a farce like *Her Cardboard Lover*, Laurette Taylor would be cavorting around and then catch you up in a moment of emotion. Without that, comedy's negligible; people can laugh and laugh and laugh, but they don't care.

LAMBERT: I take it you don't care about improvisation as such.

CUKOR: I'm quite impatient with actors who consider it an attack on their integrity if they're asked to stick to the text. If they don't really examine the lines and speak them, everything goes fuzzy. The original lines haunt them, they spend too much time faking it, the whole thing becomes inexact. Improvisation is all well and good as a parlor game, but try and do a scene with a beginning, middle and end that way. You get endless repetition and you diffuse the intensity.

LAMBERT: What about acting schools?

CUKOR: Too many young actors go to them these days, I think principally because there's not enough continuity of work in Hollywood anymore. They're kept there for years and years, and I suppose the teachers do well out of it. But it's no substitute for real experience. I don't mean that one can't study, but too few teachers seem to help actors with the useful things. The result is a lot of actors who can talk through their noses but are unable to move properly. They speak very slowly, they make the same break in every sentence, the rhythm is monotonous. . . . And while they'll talk to you a lot about their search for identity, they all seem to be searching for the same identity. I know the basic thing can't be taught—as Artur Rubinstein said, "You've got to have talent"—but you *can* learn a basic attitude toward your craft. I rather believe in modesty, myself. These intellectual pretensions give actors an overtone of being virtuous and self-righteous; they wrap around themselves this robe of being right. They can be playing a quite simple part, a reporter or a detective or something, and they behave the way lesbians used to act.

LAMBERT: You attribute all of this to training?

CUKOR: No, only partly. But I think many acting teachers in their turn have been too influenced by psychoanalysis. It seems to me that psychoanalysis says, "I am absolutely odious, I am perfectly terrible, but look at what my parents did to me. . . ." Now, when someone says, "I'm selfish," and so on, does the analyst ever tell him, "Look—try not being selfish"? Does he ever say that?

Working . . . Jane Fonda on *The Chapman Report*

Doesn't he say instead, "Of course you're selfish, *because . . . ,*" and then remove what he calls the guilt and let the patient live with it? This kind of thing haunts the air, and instead of being encouraged to overcome a weakness, a young actor has it "explained" to him and is allowed to indulge it.

LAMBERT: I think you're right, and I think it's also come from a tradition of playwriting, beginning with the Group Theatre and culminating in Arthur Miller. You know all those plays in which a character airs all his unattractiveness and problems in public and it seems to confer automatic nobility on him? If you're "honest" about yourself, you're allowed to get away with anything. You've admitted it, you've confessed it, and then you can go on being as swinish as you like.

CUKOR: I agree, but I see the influence of psychoanalysis there, too. It's basically the same point of view. And Mr. Lee Strasberg passes it on to actors.

. . . and with James Mason on *A Star Is Born*

LAMBERT: It's interesting that quite a few of the Actors Studio "stars" have never really caught on with the public.

CUKOR: You know, in her early days, after she went from musical comedy to light comedy, Ina Claire was taken by a friend to watch Bernhardt from the wings. When the show was over, Ina's friend introduced her to Bernhardt. He said, "This is one of our great young actresses." "No, no," Ina protested, "I'm just a popular actress." And Bernhardt answered, "Very well, very well. First come popular, then come great." That says it.

LAMBERT: Many of the qualities you look for in an actor can be summed up in the word "professional."

CUKOR: Oh, yes. And some actresses—more than actors, I think —after fifty years are still the eternal amateurs. They can be arty or quite intelligent but still amateurs. Like the very intellectual actresses doing Ibsen over here in the nineties.

LAMBERT: They must have been a bit bluestocking, too. It would have been at the time of the suffragettes.

CUKOR: Whatever they were, they weren't very good. Sam Behrman said that when he was writing his book on Max Beerbohm, he asked Maugham, "What sort of an actress was Lady Beerbohm?" (She was an American actress.) And Maugham said, "She-she-she's an *Ibsen* actress, which means she's an actress who can't act!" Perhaps I shouldn't say this, but I'll tell you who is the *doyenne* of this kind of thing today. Sybil Thorndike. One's *amazed* that she's been on the stage for seventy-five years. She still does dumb shows. One can't believe the naïveté of it. Then the charm and the worthiness and the greatness of the personality conquer you.

LAMBERT: And that kind of thing would never get by in movies. What you call *right up close* would expose it.

CUKOR: It's the opposite of movie acting. Lewis Milestone used to tell this story. Gary Cooper was playing with Emil Jannings in a silent picture, and Milestone, who was directing it, said to his assistant one day, "Shoot fifty feet of Gary just sitting there." As a matter of fact, Gary wasn't just sitting there, he was asleep, so they shot the footage without waking him up. Then Milestone said loudly, "Wake up!" and Gary did, and they shot this, too. Later Milestone cut Gary waking up into the picture, and when Jannings saw it, he said, "That young man should play Hamlet!"

Little Women
(1933)

CUKOR: When Selznick wanted me to do *Little Women*, I hadn't read the book. (Kate Hepburn once accused me of never having finished it, which is a lie.) Of course I'd heard of it all my life, but it was a story that little girls read, like Elsie Dinsmore. When I came to read it, I was startled. It's not sentimental or saccharine, but very strong-minded, full of character, and a wonderful picture of New England family life. It's full of that admirable New England sternness, about sacrifice and austerity. And then Kate Hepburn cast something over it. Like Garbo in *Camille*, she was born to play this part. She's tender and funny, fiercely loyal, and plays the fool when she feels like it. There's a purity about her.

LAMBERT: About the whole picture. I think it's very interesting that the book surprised you. It accounts for the sense of personal discovery and freshness in the film.

CUKOR: Yes, maybe I was able to get that feeling across. And everything went so well. The sets were done by a man called Hobe Irwin, at RKO, and he made no chi-chi. At Metro there was a lot of chi-chi. We reproduced the Louisa May Alcott house with great taste and detail. This was the beginning of my interest in research—how stimulating it could be. Walter Plunkett designed the clothes with a great sense of the family—the girls were poor but high-minded, and it was arranged that one of them would wear a certain dress at a certain time, and then another would borrow a skirt or a jacket, and so on. The frugality was very real. And we even had real snow on the RKO ranch. (Snow is something I'm very sentimental about.) The script was very right, too, and did something quite original for the time. It wasn't slicked up. The construction was very loose, very episodic, like the novel. No plottiness. Things happen, but they're not all tied together. (The later version made the mistake of slicking it up.) But the writers believed in the book, they understood its vitality, which is not namby-pamby in any way.

LAMBERT: Yes, I like the way the screenplay follows the novel's episodic quality, as in *David Copperfield*.

CUKOR: But the recent version of *David Copperfield* slicked that up, too. If you really respect a work, you must respect the weaknesses, or the vagaries, as well as the strength. For instance, the scene when Beth gets desperately sick and it looks as if she's going to die. Then she gets better. Then she gets sick again. Then she becomes an invalid. And finally, she dies. Nothing is smoothed out. And there's no love interest until the last quarter of the picture, when Jo meets the professor. And that develops very gradually, very discreetly, too. Paul Lukas was charming, wasn't he?

LAMBERT: And so right. There's something very truthful about their episodes. You believe that Jo, for all her high spirits and charm, has something spinsterish in her character, and that she would choose to marry a middle-aged, fatherly, slightly dull man. You believe it.

CUKOR: Another thing about the construction. People used to say, "I liked the way you handled that big scene." And I'd ask, "What big scene, what big scene?" And they had different ideas which the big scenes were. Well, I didn't feel any of them were big scenes. I never thought in terms of "famous climaxes" and all that. It would have betrayed the whole approach.

LAMBERT: You don't betray anything, and you don't flinch from anything. There's a moment toward the end when Jo suddenly addresses her dead sister "up there in the sky." Razor's edge stuff, and it works completely. No tear-jerking, no apology for it. In the same way, the family accepts hardship and sacrifice as a matter of course. They're never self-consciously noble, they never congratulate each other.

CUKOR: That moment you mention got at you because by this time Kate Hepburn had cast a spell of magic and a kind of power over the picture. You could go with whatever she did. She really felt it all very deeply. She's a New England girl who understands all that and has her own family feeling.

LAMBERT: Although she's so good, and in a way dominates the film, the others come up to her.

CUKOR: Yes, Frances Dee as the elder sister, and a little girl I hadn't heard of before, Jean Parker—both very good. And Joan Bennett—I saw her at a party and she was a little tight, and I thought, "Oh yes!" She was very sweet and funny, and absolutely right, so we cast her.

LAMBERT: The only disappointment is Spring Byington as the mother.

CUKOR: I don't remember why we cast her. She's not at all the way Louisa May Alcott describes her, the "tall, stately lady." She's too one-dimensional, plays at "loving her children" in the wrong way.

LAMBERT: I see a connection between *Little Women* and *The Actress*—a similarity of tone and the feeling for family life.

CUKOR (*very surprised*): Really?! (*Pause*) Well, yes. They're both New England, and the people have the same kind of strong-mindedness and austerity.

LAMBERT: And they're both deceptively simple films. No obvious effects, no big scenes.

CUKOR: I know I always say this, but the text determined that. You couldn't have done either picture in any other style. The director must never overwhelm a picture, he must serve it. This may not be the most attention-getting way, but I believe in it. The moment you're aware of something, like the photography is so great, it usually means something else is lacking. Look at Truffaut's *Stolen Kisses*. A wonderful picture that never hits you over the head with anything. Unless you really looked very closely, very professionally, you weren't aware how discreet and right the setups were, they were so unobtrusive. But d'you think young people would understand the motivation of *Little Women* today?

[77]

On location for *Little Women*: Douglass Montgomery,
Katharine Hepburn, Cukor gestures

Little Women: Jean Parker (Beth), Katharine Hepburn (Jo), Spring
Byington (Mother), Joan Bennett (Amy), Frances Dee (Meg)

Katharine Hepburn
as Jo

Wouldn't they want one of the girls to be fighting for civil rights or something? Wouldn't they think them square for being grateful for what they had?

LAMBERT: All I can tell you is, I screened the picture with a group of young cinema students, and they were entranced by it. All its ideas about family life and discipline may be the complete antithesis of how many young people feel now, but the emotion got through to them. Purity is the word. The way you and Hepburn believed in the picture is irresistible. No false notes. People always respond to that. I can well understand why it's your own favorite picture.

LAMBERT: After *Little Women*, you were firmly established as what they call a "leading Hollywood director." Did you feel by then that the pattern of your career, the kind of director you were going to be, was now up to you? I mean by this, did you decide to accept assignments that appealed to you, material you felt you could do well and through which you were going to express yourself? Or did you think about initiating projects of your own, going after things, saying "I must do this"?

CUKOR: At that time the practice of directors setting up their own projects hadn't started. For one thing, the companies bought up all the best material. It wasn't until later that people came up with their own projects.

LAMBERT: But when, say, Metro had bought a property and you wanted to do it, did you go after it?

CUKOR: No. I had that curious feeling, if it was for me, I'd get it. I never played any politics. That was rather naïve of me, I suppose.

LAMBERT: Well, it worked a lot of the time. But you never had the feeling that a particular story that the studio owned was something you burned to do and that you had to try and get assigned to it?

CUKOR: Once or twice I proposed myself. I read a book and said, "Yes, I can do this." Or rather, "I think I can do this uniquely well." Once I wanted to do a story called *Escape*, an anti-Nazi thing. I proposed myself but they'd assigned it to someone else. Besides, all those years I worked at Metro, Louis B. Mayer never really liked me.

LAMBERT: Why was that? You directed so many successful pictures for Metro.

CUKOR: I don't know. I was brought into Metro by Selznick, at that time Mayer's son-in-law. He didn't think of me as his own man. I think my manner seemed to be frivolous and hard-bitten and New York-sophisticated. They cast directors, you know, like actors. Frank Borzage did *Seventh Heaven* and they labeled him a romantic director. My first film at Metro was *Dinner at Eight*, so they pegged me as New York wise guy. Then, when I made *David Copperfield* for them, I found myself in a costume period. I had to pull myself out of that. (Today, I suppose, I have to pull myself out of being "establishment.") Of course, there have always been certain things I've had no sympathy for, like gangster pictures, and I've always turned them down.

LAMBERT: Perhaps in one sense you've been very lucky. Hollywood has nearly always had something to offer that you wanted to do. It interested you to film plays like *A Bill of Divorcement* and *Dinner at Eight*, it developed your instinct for working with actors. And then *David Copperfield* began a phase of period pictures, which also interested you. After that, with *Holiday* and *Philadelphia Story*, the fashion for sophisticated comedy brought out something else new. . . .

CUKOR: Yes, I consider myself lucky. (*Firmly*) And I was good! I never just latched onto what was going around, you know. If I did, I'd be going around on motorcycles right now and being very soulful.

LAMBERT: Still, there was never a period when there was nothing around that you wanted to do.

CUKOR: No. Although recently they've kept on saying to me about something I've proposed, "But it's not youth-orientated."

LAMBERT: Isn't that partly an economic problem? Money's tight, they're making much fewer pictures here, the atmosphere is very uncertain.

CUKOR: Yes, but they're taking the pulse and the temperature of the public much too narrowly, too immediately now. That's a bad way to go. The catch-as-catch-can approach wears itself out, people start getting bored. I know that you can't go back to the well-made thing, that the public is very educated and on to all sorts of things. I like that myself. I don't mind being baffled and asking myself at first, "What is it?" But I still believe the only way is to ask, "Do I want to do that?" and if I do, to believe I can make it vivid enough to get it across to an audience.

David Copperfield
(1935)

CUKOR: David Selznick had this habit of making a list of all the possible classics he might one day want to film and registering the titles with the Producers' Association. Then, unless he produced a particular title within a certain time, it went back on the open market. (This was just an agreement among the producers themselves.) Anyway, he finally picked *David Copperfield* from the list and asked me to do it with him at Metro. Louis B. Mayer thought the boy should be played by Jackie Cooper. "He's a big star," he said, "and a marvelously appealing child." David and I dug in our heels and told him we couldn't have any American boy, however appealing, to play such a famous English laddie. We won our point and found Freddie Bartholomew, who was perfect, except that he had a British schoolboy's *noblesse oblige* and it was terribly difficult to make him cry. It's a pity that in the book David Copperfield grows up to be such a bore, a typical young Victorian—people chided me about this when they saw the picture and said, "The second half is not as good as the first." "Well," I said, "the second volume of the novel is not as good as the first."

By then I'd discovered my own rule in doing adaptations, which I've told you about: You must get the essence of the original, which may involve accepting some of the weaknesses. When you read *David Copperfield* you know why it's lasted. There's too much melodrama and the second half is unsatisfactory, but there's this underlying vitality and invention. For me, that determined the style of the picture. In the same way, there was the problem of re-creating Dickens' characters, making them slightly grotesque, at times caricature, yet completely human—as Dickens did himself. It was a difficult thing, making these people funny and frightening at the same time. You achieve it partly by the casting but also by deciding on the style of playing. The outward semblance is important, too, and here we were guided by Phiz, who did the original illustrations. And somehow I think we managed all that.

LAMBERT: Real and exaggerated at the same time—that's the key to your film and its success. You had this response to the essence of Dickens, which is why I find *David Copperfield* the truest Dickens film ever made. It comes from the inside, the opposite method to David Lean's in *Great Expectations*, which is quite brilliant but somehow exterior. You have the feeling that Lean tried to scale down Dickens and in a very intelligent way to accommodate him to what he thought the demands of a modern audience would be. You didn't bother with that. You trusted your own reaction to the original, assuming that if it had lasted this long it had to be all right.

CUKOR: How that managed to get on the screen one doesn't exactly know. Research has a good deal to do with it, too. I told you that on *Little Women* I discovered for the first time how stimulating the process of research could be.

LAMBERT: Although the picture was shot in Hollywood, I imagine you went to England to research?

CUKOR: Yes, after winning our point with Mayer, we went off there—David and myself and the writer, Howard Estabrook. Various literary people gave us a welcoming lunch when we arrived—Hugh Walpole, J. B. Priestley, and for some reason John Masefield—and then we got in touch with the head of the Dickens Society. He told us about every place associated with the novel, and we went there and took pictures. We photographed Betsy Trotwood's house and the White Cliffs of Dover. (But we shot the Dover scenes in California, near Malibu, and I have to say *our* cliffs were better—whiter and cliffier.) I found all this intensely stimulating. The result of research is never quite what you expect. That's why I do it. When you really *look* at things, you reeducate your eyes and your sensibilities.

LAMBERT: While you were in England, Hugh Walpole came in on the script. How did that happen?

CUKOR: Estabrook had laid out the whole structure. Then we thought Walpole would be good to write the dialogue. He didn't know anything about screen technique, but he understood Dickens and the tone that we needed. He also played a small part in the picture, the parson. His father had been a bishop in New Zealand, and Hugh was very good at imitating long sermons— although when we tried to shoot close-ups he got self-conscious.

David Copperfield: David (Freddie Bartholomew), Mr. Dick (Lennox Pawle), Aunt Betsey (Edna May Oliver), Mr. Murdstone (Basil Rathbone), Mrs. Murdstone (Violet Kemble-Cooper)

Micawber (W. C. Fields)
and David

The Dickensian mother:
Elizabeth Allan as
Mrs. Copperfield

He was a darling fellow and rather terrified of Somerset Maugham, who was quite cutting about him. But he had great humor and genuine modesty, and he looked the way a distinguished English writer is supposed to look. He made a real contribution, not in dramatic terms but in giving us the right sound for the characters.

LAMBERT: Did you shoot anything in England at all?

CUKOR: We used only one second-unit shot, a charming shot of the young David walking to Canterbury.

LAMBERT: There were so many good British character actors in Hollywood at that time. Did you have to bring any over?

CUKOR: No, we were very lucky. Roland Young not only managed to look like Uriah Heep, he really *performed* like him. Elizabeth Allan made an adorable Mrs. Copperfield, and Basil Rathbone and Violet Kemble Cooper made a wonderful pair of Murdstones. We had a problem at first with Micawber. I wanted Charles Laughton, who wasn't keen to do it, but we persuaded him. He devised a marvelous makeup and *looked* perfect, but it turned out he just didn't have the geniality or the innocence for the part. We got on very well—in spite of his strange habits, such as a terrific prejudice concerning Jews and needing strange offstage noises to get himself in the mood for acting. He was the first actor I encountered who prepared to make a laughing entrance by going around doing *ha-ha!* sounds for hours. But it didn't work out. We shot for about a week, then he withdrew.

LAMBERT: And you got W. C. Fields. In spite of being an outsider in the cast, he worked brilliantly.

CUKOR: He was really born to play it, even though he'd never played a real character role before—that rare combination of the personality and the part.

LAMBERT: Were there any problems in Fields' having been an act rather than an actor?

CUKOR: He was charming to work with, his suggestions and ad libs were always in character. There was a scene in which he had to sit at a desk writing, and he asked me if he could have a cup of tea on the desk. When he got agitated, he dipped his pen into the teacup instead of the inkwell. Another time he was sitting on a high stool and asked for a wastepaper basket so he could get his feet stuck in it. Physically he wasn't quite right, wasn't bald as Dickens describes Micawber—but his spirit was perfect.

LAMBERT: Nearly all the performances are perfect. The only one I question is Lionel Barrymore as Dan Peggotty—he pushes too hard. And, then, the art direction strikes me as uneven. It seems to hover between two styles, realistic and artificial. The more artificial it is, the better—like the shipwreck scene and the stylized streets.

CUKOR: There were problems. I wanted *everything* more stylized, less solid than the kind of thing the studio preferred. But they pressured us, and in that way the picture was less successful than *Little Women*.

LAMBERT: In spite of that, the movie charms because its feeling is so right. What finally matters in Dickens are the people.

CUKOR: When the picture came out, it ran over two hours—which was very long for those days. Some people reproached us for letting it run on, not organizing it more. But when the remake came out recently, most people said how right we were after all. Well, as I told you, I don't believe in "correcting" Dickens, "saving" him and all that. I just had to go with the vitality of the thing.

Interlude:
On David O. Selznick

CUKOR: The thing that bothers me in talking about
David is that everything I say might be interpreted
today, because of our differences on *Gone with the
Wind*, as critical. I don't want to be critical. We were
friends very early on, and he helped me greatly, and
we worked very well together, and in spite of vicissitudes we
remained friends. I remained friends with his first wife Irene, too,
and became a friend of Jennifer's. We rode out so many things
together. . . . About *Gone with the Wind*—I really can't tell you
why. There came a point, after I'd been shooting for a few weeks,
when he obviously didn't think I could do it. I'd spent a year on
it before shooting, making tests—but a great many people on that
project failed to last. Sidney Howard was taken off the script—

LAMBERT: Weren't there innumerable writers? Including, for
about a week, Scott Fitzgerald?

CUKOR: Endless writers, just endless writers, and I believe very
briefly Fitzgerald. But David somehow kept the whole thing in
his head and stuck with it. Then a story went around that Clark

Gable had never really wanted me. It may or may not be true. I honestly don't know. Perhaps Gable mistakenly thought that because I was supposed to be a "woman's director" I would throw the story to Vivien—but if that's so, it was very naïve of him and not the reaction of a very good or professional actor. It's not the director who "throws" things and puts the emphasis the wrong way. That would be like singing a song, and singing certain notes very loudly or heavily to divert attention from the others. I don't throw anything anywhere at all; there's the truth of the scene and it states itself. But as I say, I don't know for sure. Gable was always very polite with me.

LAMBERT: How much of what you shot remains in the picture?

CUKOR: Practically everything. There are two quite long, completed scenes: early in the war, when Scarlett is nursing Melanie through her labor pains and has to deal with the frightened, hysterical servant, Butterfly McQueen; and after the war, when the marauding soldier breaks into Tara and Scarlett copes with him.

LAMBERT: Your relationship with Selznick began so well. All those pictures—*What Price Hollywood?, Dinner at Eight, Little Women, David Copperfield*—

CUKOR: Yes, originally it was very happy. He was the producer I respected, I was a director he had some regard for. Then, as things went on, he seemed to trust me less. He wanted to attend the rehearsals of *Gone with the Wind*, which I thought unwise. I was the director, after all, and a director should shoot the scene before the producer sees it. That's when the producer's opinion is important, when he sees it on the screen for the first time. And then David started coming down on the set, giving hot tips which weren't really very helpful. He'd never done that before. He changed our method of working. Naturally he was in on the whole thing, casting and script and sets and costumes, but this time he seemed to want to be in on the direction as well. Although the picture finally came off very effectively and successfully, I think it contained the seeds of his destruction.

LAMBERT: Especially when they have big successes, producers want to direct and say they can do it better—but for some reason they don't take the actual step, so it frustrates them and spoils their relationship with directors.

CUKOR: And yet it had never been that way before. Afterward, on another picture, didn't David and John Huston have a row; didn't John Huston leave?

LAMBERT: That was *A Farewell to Arms*.

CUKOR: It was really sad. David's great strength had been his relationship with people, and somehow it began to fall apart. All his stars left him. Ingrid left him, then there was a lawsuit with Vivien Leigh. It seemed to chip away at his whole base. Yet he remained, outside of working with him, as sweet and kind and interesting as ever. He just became one, alas, who couldn't go with the times. The empire seemed to float away. From time to time he'd talk about another project with me, and it would always be something like, "Why don't we do *The Letter* again?" As the times changed, he seemed to lean more and more back to the past. He started to remake, with very poor results, *Little Women*. . . . Yet he remained a generous man who would always go to any trouble for a friend, a tough businessman with a big streak of personal tenderness and loyalty. In spite of *Gone with the Wind*, I felt no bitterness toward him. When something like that happens, it's the luck of the game. But when you've finished a picture and it's ruined by other people's cutting, that's much worse, and it stays with you.

Sylvia Scarlett
(1935)

LAMBERT: This picture stands quite apart from your others in the thirties. Have you seen it again recently?

CUKOR: Not in a long time.

LAMBERT: I wonder why there was such a terrific controversy over something very charming and very lightweight.

CUKOR: I'm not putting *Sylvia Scarlett* in the same class, but when *Carmen* was first done at the Opéra Comique they picked up their chairs and threw them at the stage.

LAMBERT: But this is just a simple, mildly eccentric tale of a girl who disguises herself as a boy to help out her dear old father, who's a thief and a con man, and both men and women fall in love with him/her. The violence of the reaction—

CUKOR: Oh, Kate and I fostered that. We emphasized it. Actually the picture just wasn't very successful, it was kind of passed over.

LAMBERT: After being a commercial flop, it disappeared for years, then it began to acquire an underground reputation, and now it's a minor cult film.

CUKOR: It had a remarkable vitality and it's survived all kinds of things. Even after it was passed over, it kept on playing in little theaters for years, and I'd use it as an insanity test. When people said to me—Judy Holliday said it once—"Oh, I loved that picture!" I used to tell them, "Now I know about *you,* your mind is not too good." It was a lost cause for many years. I suppose that for Kate and myself, our attitude has frozen into being comic about it.

LAMBERT: At the time you made it did you think of it as daring?

CUKOR: I don't remember what I thought. I'd always liked the book, and it struck me that Kate had that quality they used to call *garçonne,* and I thought it would be a perfect part for her.

LAMBERT: So it was your own liking for the book that started the project?

CUKOR: Yes, I took it to RKO, and they said, "All right, do it." It seemed an impertinent thing to do, but I didn't realize how daring. . . . (*His manner wavers between affection and regret.*) But then we got John Collier for the script, and he was a daring kind of writer, so I suppose I *must* have been thinking in that way. (*Pause*) But the picture did something to me. It slowed me up. I wasn't going to be so goddamned daring after that. I thought, "Well, kiddo, don't you break all sorts of new paths, you just watch it."

LAMBERT: You really made up your mind to play it safe?

CUKOR: Yes.

LAMBERT: The generally hostile reaction didn't strike you as unfair?

CUKOR: When you're clobbered on the head, it's difficult to remember your exact feelings. Anyway, I lack the nerve and the confidence to indulge myself in self-pity. I just thought, "Christ, you'd better get on with something else." Isn't there something very healthy and bouncy about that? Anyway, it wasn't the daring part of *Sylvia Scarlett* that failed, I see that now. It was when we tried to play it safe!

LAMBERT: The last fifteen minutes?

CUKOR: And the prologue.

LAMBERT: The opening scene? After her mother has died—and she cuts off her hair to sell it?

CUKOR: Yes, that was put in later. It was never intended. We

"Picaresque right here in Laurel Canyon!" Katharine Hepburn,
Cukor, Cary Grant on the *Sylvia Scarlett* location

started originally with Kate and her father, Edmund Gwenn, on board the ship from France to England—she's already disguised as a boy—and they meet up with Cary Grant, who's also in the swindling business.

LAMBERT: Was the prologue tacked on as a sympathy device? Poor girl—her mother died and what else could she do?

CUKOR: Something like that. Now what exactly happens in the last fifteen minutes?

LAMBERT: Plot. It gets very plotty. Wheels start turning to get Hepburn away from Grant and back to her true love, the artist played by Brian Aherne.

CUKOR (*rather amused*): Oh, yes. Doesn't Natalie Paley, Aherne's old girlfriend, go into the water and almost drown?

LAMBERT: Yes, and Hepburn rescues her.

CUKOR: But all that had nothing to do with the rest of it at all!

LAMBERT: No. Up to then the picture's very free as far as plot is concerned. (I suppose that put people off at the time, too.) It's very loosely constructed, things just happen, you're not quite sure where you're going—the word, I suppose, is picaresque.

CUKOR: Picaresque right here in Laurel Canyon. The whole thing was done up in the hills! Wasn't it pretty?

LAMBERT: Very pretty, and it looks very English.

CUKOR: We shot the White Cliffs of Dover beyond Malibu, the same place we used for Betsy Trotwood's house in *David Copperfield*. Joe August was the cameraman. I thought his work was very strong and outdoorsy. (*Pause*) Picaresque or whatever it was, they loathed it.

LAMBERT: But I'm sure, as you said, that playing it safe at the beginning and the end had a lot to do with that. It's the old story: Don't lose heart when you've got something unconventional; stick with it.

CUKOR: Yes, we shouldn't have lost heart. . . . And yet I always felt a lot of it was very good. When they join up with the traveling players, and there's a rural pagan feast, a bacchanal, and Teddy Gwenn is dressed up as a satyr. . . .

LAMBERT: A lovely sequence.

CUKOR: I suppose there were important things that failed, and that's why it failed as a whole.

LAMBERT: I like very much the way you played on the sexual

Sylvia Scarlett; Hepburn,
Brian Aherne

Moment of decision:
Hepburn as *Sylvia
Scarlett*

LADIES
DAMES

misunderstandings. When Brian Aherne is attracted to Hepburn as a boy and worried about it, he says, "There's something very queer going on here."

CUKOR: I don't remember that. It's funny.

LAMBERT: And then the maid finds Hepburn a very attractive boy and makes love to her.

CUKOR: I remember that. All that kind of thing is in the classical tradition, of course.

LAMBERT: Do you think moments like that shocked people when the picture first came out?

CUKOR: No. They just didn't think it was funny.

LAMBERT: Hepburn is wonderful in the part, as you'd expect, but the interesting revelation is Cary Grant, as a kind of humorous leading man.

CUKOR: You see, up to then Cary had been a conventional leading man. This part was extremely well written, and he knew this kind of raffish life, he'd been a stilt-walker in a circus. And he'd had enough experience by this time to know what he was up to, and suddenly this part hit him, and he felt the ground under his feet.

LAMBERT: In 1935 how serious was it to have made a picture that flopped?

CUKOR: Well, it wasn't pleasant. It didn't really injure me—I think it injured Kate much more. But I certainly didn't like it.

LAMBERT: While you were making it, you didn't have any inkling of disaster? As you did later with *Two-Faced Woman*?

CUKOR: Oh, no. But Kate said afterward that halfway through she began losing confidence in the material. She thought that I did, too, though she never asked me. I found certain scenes very difficult to do. When they don't play themselves—to use that old cliché—it's very worrying. A good scene somehow falls into place and carries itself and you and everything else with it.

LAMBERT: Wasn't the preview a famous disaster?

CUKOR: A nightmare. People rushing out up the aisles! Then Kate went into the ladies' john, and there was a woman lying down there. Kate asked, "Was the picture so bad?" and the woman just raised her eyes up to heaven. . . . Then we got into my car, and Kate hit her head—I had a low car in those days—and she said, "Thank God I've knocked myself out." And we came back here, to this house, and Pan Berman, the producer, was already here. And Kate and I said, "Pandro, scrap the picture, we'll do another picture for you for nothing!" (*Amused*) And *he* said, not kidding, "I never want to see either of you again!" So it wasn't very pleasant. But, listen, we've both had many kicks in the ass since.

Interlude:
On Katharine Hepburn

CUKOR: Kate and I have been friends and collaborators for forty years, and as she once remarked, there's nothing she could now say to me that would disturb me, and vice versa. It's amusing to go back to that first day when she walked into my office at RKO after Selznick and I had signed her for *A Bill of Divorcement*. She struck me as completely in command of herself from the first moment, although *her* version now is that she was absolutely petrified and feeling ill and her eyes were red. I remember showing her the costume sketches for the character, and she didn't like them and said so at once, which was typical. She told me that no well-bred English girl would wear clothes like that and began talking about Chanel. I got my own back by criticizing what she had on—it was expensive but I thought it stank, and I said so—and then taking her to the makeup department to have her hair cut. When we began shooting the picture, she had this remarkable assurance that I've mentioned before. During the scene with Jack Barrymore that you told me you liked—when he comes home and she watches him from the stairs—I discovered later that she

Hepburn prepares (*The Philadelphia Story*)

thought on the first take he was doing too much. She looked at this famous actor with "the cold eye of youth," as she called it, and made her own evaluation. Imagine, it was the first scene she had to play with him, on her first picture, and she was able to think this, and hide what she was thinking, and act away during the take! Another time, during the shooting, she said to me, "Just because you don't know what you're doing, don't take it out on us!" You've got to be naturally tough with yourself to be so tough with other people. When she met Tallulah, "your friend Miss Bankhead," as she called her, she criticized her to me for using too much bad language. . . . Once, during *Little Women*, I actually hit Kate. (Not hard enough, probably.) She had to run up a flight of steps carrying some ice cream, and I told her to be very careful because we didn't have a spare of the dress she was wearing, so she *mustn't* spill that ice cream. But she did and ruined the dress, and then she laughed—and I hit her and called her an amateur. But, of course, she was immensely professional. During *Little Women* some of the sound men were on strike, and we had

George Hoyningen-Huene with Katharine Hepburn

a makeshift, inexperienced crew, and Kate had to do take after take of a very emotional scene simply because the sound men kept messing it up. After the fifteenth take, or whatever, they got it— and Kate was so exhausted and agonized by all that weeping, she threw up. But not *until* we'd got the take. There's a lot of Kate herself in some of the pictures we did together, and you'll find different views of her character in the impatient anti-establishment young girl of *A Bill of Divorcement*, the New England side in *Little Women*, independent and idealistic, and in *The Philadelphia Story* the self-willed, apparently high and mighty heroine who's a great romantic at heart. Later, when I worked with her and Spencer Tracy together, it was a fascinating combination of opposites. Kate says I was always giving *her* hundreds of suggestions but none to Spence. Well, Spence was the kind of actor about whom you thought, "I've got a lot of things I could say to you, but I don't say them because you *know*," and next day everything I'd thought of telling him would be there in the rushes. Also, I was never sure whether Spence was really listening when I talked to him. He was one of those naturally original actors who did it but never let you see him doing it. Kate is one of those originals with a lot of ideas she likes to tell you about. So on *Adam's Rib* and *Pat and Mike* Spence never joined the script conferences, whereas Kate and I worked with Ruth and Garson Kanin and alone by ourselves all the way through. An original does things in his own way, and you've got to learn it. It's the same thing with friendship. You learn when to talk and when to leave people alone. But in one way Spence and Kate weren't opposites at all. The very best actors never talk very much about acting itself—and above all they never talk about it until they've done it. Real talent is a mystery, and people who've got it know it.

Romeo and Juliet
(1936)

CUKOR: This one has fallen into great disrepute now. Maybe we made it too stately?

LAMBERT: I think so. Zeffirelli discovered something very important about the play both on the stage and when he made it into a film. It works much better when the lovers are really young.

CUKOR: I found Zeffirelli's picture very imperfect but full of pep and life—and it was certainly fascinating that he managed to engage young people so much. But I thought many of the actors spoke their lines so badly. Was that any better in his stage production?

LAMBERT: In the case of Romeo, yes—a young actor from the Old Vic called John Stryde. Whoever played Juliet had one of those ultra-British virginal voices, more classical, I suppose, but much less lively than Olivia Hussey in the film.

CUKOR: Somebody said that Zeffirelli's Juliet sounded like a chemist's daughter from Wimbledon. I agree the film was a damn good show, but I didn't believe either Romeo or Juliet as coming

Cukor lining up a shot with Norma Shearer in the
ballroom scene from *Romeo and Juliet*

from the nobility. They were just nice, sexy kids who carried on
like mad. But then maybe *our* lovers were too stodgy.

LAMBERT: Your picture seemed to me too inhibited by the
concept at the time of "cultural prestige." It's short on passion,
though often very attractive to look at. Had you been thinking
about pre-Raphaelite paintings before you made it? Norma
Shearer's Juliet in particular looks like someone out of Burne-
Jones.

CUKOR: No, Oliver Messel did the sets, and he and Adrian did
the costumes, some of which were copied from Botticelli. I certainly think—and this was probably my fault—there should have
been a more Italian, Mediterranean look to the thing. It's not
desperate enough. Zeffirelli got that very well.

LAMBERT: Norma Shearer told me how intimidated she was by

the part. The whole English theatrical tradition impressed her very much, and she knew she didn't belong to it.

CUKOR: Neither she nor Leslie Howard were really passionate actors. But I thought she did the potion scene wonderfully, and Leslie's last speech was very fine.

LAMBERT: The picture is the opposite of *David Copperfield*—more concerned to *be* a classic than find the essence of a classic.

CUKOR: It was unfamiliar territory for me, I suppose. It's one picture that if I had to do over again, I'd know how. I'd get the garlic and the Mediterranean into it. And then there was a tug of war about the way the picture should look. (I never got my way about how a costume picture should look at Metro until *Camille*.) On one side there was Adrian and the resident M-G-M art director, Cedric Gibbons. On the other there was Oliver Messel. Irving Thalberg sat like Solomon and never committed himself. I wanted to go with Oliver, but I didn't succeed in breaking the barrier. The result is what you see, neither one thing nor the other. It's original at moments—like the ball scene, with Agnes de Mille's choreography—and conventional at others.

LAMBERT: Were Messel's ideas constantly modified by the studio's art department?

CUKOR: You see, the studio was very successful at this time and had its own way of doing things. They bullied Messel and said he didn't know anything about pictures. Mind you, since that time I've learned to cope with situations like that—I just don't listen at all. . . . The big studios had certain disadvantages as well as enormous things in their favor, and in this case I should have been more definite, more combative. I'm not apologizing—either for this or for a few details in *Camille* that weren't exactly right. I'm only saying that if I'd been more forceful, we'd have arrived at something better.

Interlude:
On Showmen

CUKOR: Louis B. Mayer knew that the coin he dealt in was talent. He would husband it and be very patient with it and put up with an awful lot of nonsense if he really believed in it. Of course, he was tough, and he could be ruthless and very disagreeable, but all the recent books about him and Harry Cohn and the others represent the great showmen simply as monsters—and that's stupid. In Mayer's case, the proof is that he and Thalberg built up this extraordinary concentration of talent which was M-G-M, and when Mayer left the whole studio began going to pot. I think people don't understand how a place like M-G-M had to be fed, sustained and organized every day. The organization was really wonderful. It was so convenient to work there, a marvelous research department, a marvelous foreign department that could tell you about the rights on a European property within forty-eight hours. . . .

LAMBERT: Mayer would seem to have had a nose not only for the obvious talent but the more unlikely kind. Didn't he support

[105]

Garbo, whose films really brought in more prestige than money?

CUKOR: Oh, yes. They were a strange mixture, these men. They were rough and tough but had a natural discretion. They loathed vulgarity! Isn't that extraordinary? They were very careful about nudity and coarseness on the screen—not because of the censors but because they didn't like it. Harry Cohn and Jack Warner both hated women to wear "obvious" clothes. And they were showmen who didn't need popularity polls or Nielsen ratings. They made their decisions and stuck by them. They had complete confidence. Thalberg was very creative, but tough as well. Physically he looked fragile, and in fact he was, but he was capable of enormous work. He wasn't well educated, but he was far from ignorant. He had a kind of instinct for refinement.

LAMBERT: I heard a very shrewd thing he said about Garbo. He thought that in her films she was best when things happened to her, rather than when she made things happen.

CUKOR: Yes, he liked her to ride the situation. And he was right. Her career was developed under his aegis, yet he was always quite shy with her. He came on the set of *Camille* one day, and she was preoccupied, so he said, "Well, I've been turned off better sets than this," and left with the greatest grace. He looked and behaved like a prince. I didn't read that recent book about him, or the one about David Selznick. That kind of book never seems to be about the person I knew.

LAMBERT: Wasn't Thalberg fascinated by artists, as if he wanted to crack their secret?

CUKOR: Well, in his own way he was an artist himself. He was very friendly with a great many talented people. He admired them, and at the same time he was very demanding of them. He wouldn't stop until he felt everything was as good as it could possibly be. Metro was really built on that attitude. You might not always agree with what they did, but they did it so well! Thalberg died when he was thirty-seven, and I'd just started shooting *Camille*. After the picture was finished, Eddie Mannix, a top executive at the studio, called me up and said, "This will be Irving's last picture, is there anything you can do to improve it in any way?" I didn't really think there *was* by then, but I was very touched, so I did a couple of days' extra work that wasn't really needed.

LAMBERT: Is that an example of what they used to call studio loyalty?

CUKOR: Yes, but not in a theoretical way. It was a genuinely personal thing. (*Rather surprised*) It was the way we really felt at that time!

Camille
(1936)

CUKOR: Irving Thalberg was going to do two pictures with Garbo, and he offered me a choice between them. One was *Marie Walewska*, with Napoleon as the leading man. Well, Napoleon absolutely stumps me! He's fascinating to read about, but he's a Great Man—and they all come out like waxworks in the movies, even American patriots. So I chose *Camille*. I'd seen the play, and I felt it would be a perfect meeting of the actress and the role. Certain people are born to play certain parts. (I'd never worked with Garbo, but I knew her slightly.) The play presented some enormous problems, because you had to make a modern audience understand its conventions. It came from a time when a woman's reputation, her virtue, was a terribly important thing—and a big bonanza for drama. (Nowadays it's the opposite—it's a woman's freedom, her liberation.) An audience had to understand the distinction they made in those days between a "good" and a "bad" woman, especially in that scene when Armand's father tells Marguerite Gautier in a very high-handed, moral way how she's ruining his boy's life and she must give him up. (A lot of women *do* ruin men's lives, mind you, but now the fathers try and pay them off or something, or the couple runs away and gets married and has children and ruin their lives *that* way.) Anyway, the period fascinated me. In dealing with period things, the trick is not to violate the period and yet not to fall into the trap of being pretty-pretty or artificial and lifeless.

LAMBERT: Doesn't it start with your own response to the period?

CUKOR: Yes, but you have to decide on the style. How "modern" is your dialogue going to be? What kind of speech will the actors use? Today it's almost impossible to make period pictures because not enough actors know how to talk. They have to get English actors to play American parts of any distinction, and that's awfully sad. There used to be a kind of international speech in American films, unaccented because a local accent is intrusive. . . . We had problems getting the right script, and after a couple of people had tried it, Zoë Akins did a new one from scratch. She managed to create a whole language, a kind of argot for the story. She wrote one very good scene of a party at Marguerite's house. All these tarts were sitting around, and Zoë had the idea they told rather coarse jokes in front of each other and Armand was shocked by it. In the middle of all these tarts being so raucous and common, Marguerite has a coughing spell. It was the only time she really coughed in the film. Most of the time she suggested her tuberculosis by little dry clearings of the throat and touching her mouth. Most ladies cough and splutter their way through this part.

LAMBERT: Like Dustin Hoffman in *Midnight Cowboy*.

CUKOR: Yes. What Garbo did in that scene was she suddenly lost her breath and went into the other room. Armand comes in and he's revolted by the coarseness he's just heard, and I'll never forget how beautifully Garbo played the next moment. She has a line that Zoë Akins wrote—"Oh, I'm just a girl like all the rest"— as if to warn him not to put her on a pedestal and sentimentalize her. And then, later, she did this memorable erotic thing. She didn't touch Armand, but she kissed him all over his face. That's how you create eroticism. It's the uncensored thought the actor flashes to the audience. Garbo had this rapport with an audience, she could let them know she was thinking things, and thinking them uncensored. There was no "body contact" in that scene,

Camille: Garbo moods

"Some tender young man and some coughing young woman . . ." Garbo and Robert Taylor in *Camille*

which didn't matter. Garbo had that other quality in her character, and without it you can't generate a real love scene. She was rather cool, but seething underneath. You know that she's reckless and nothing will stop her; she has those fires underneath. . . . I want to tell you, too, how you achieve certain moments by really *assaulting* them. At a script conference with Zoë and Irving Thalberg we were discussing the scene when Marguerite and Armand are planning to get married. Thalberg said, "They should play this scene as though they were plotting a murder!" That was a very interesting idea, and if you remember the scene, it had a kind of tension and no sentimentality at all. Sentimentality instead of true sentiment, that was always the pitfall. The big trap in a story like this was to be sentimental. You had to find the real feeling and let it come through.

LAMBERT: Garbo has a quality in *Camille*, which she also has in life, that I don't think ever came out in her other films—her coquettishness.

CUKOR: Yes, she was gay and funny. Irving Thalberg knew her very well—he created her whole career in this country, and he died very soon after we started shooting—and he saw the early rushes of the scene at the theater where she was just sitting in a box. And he said, "She's never been quite like that, she's never been as good!" I said, "Irving, how can you possibly tell? She's just sitting there." He said, "I know, but she's *unguarded*." And I remember the very first day of shooting, when one's always nervous. I wanted to show that Marguerite was a public woman, she went to the theater to be seen. She had to walk through a crowded lobby full of men wearing hats (which they always did at the theater in those days—you can see it in contemporary prints). I wanted her to walk through to show herself, as if on parade for her clients. At first Garbo walked through rather quickly, as if she didn't want to be seen. I *might* have said, "Walk through a little more brazenly, a little more slowly"—but I didn't. I realized she was right. She could slip through, and you'd know damn well the men would look at her anyway. Now I want to read you something by Henry James. . . .

(A book is brought from the library. Cukor at once finds what he wants in it.)

He wrote this after the death of Dumas *fils*. "Written at the age of twenty-five, *La Dame aux Camélias* remains in its combination of freshness and form, of the feeling of the springtime of life and a sense of the conditions of the theatre, a singular and astonishing production. The author has had no time to part with his illusions, but he has had full opportunity to master the most difficult of the arts. The play has been blown about the world at a fearful rate, but has never lost its happy juvenility, a charm that nothing can vulgarize. . . . It is all champagne and tears, fresh perversity, fresh credulity, fresh passion, fresh pain, we've seen it both well done and ill done. . . . Nothing makes any difference. It carries with it an April air, some tender young man and some coughing young woman has only to speak the lines to give it a great place among the love stories of the world."

LAMBERT: "Champagne and tears" describes your film perfectly. Was working with Garbo particularly different, or difficult, as opposed to other actresses you've worked with?

CUKOR: No. She's extremely sensible and practical. She says what she wants, and it's very fair and based on common sense. She doesn't play tricks. For example, she always quit at five o'clock,

Directing Robert Taylor ("fresh credulity") and Garbo

which seemed a great extravagance, but I know it took her that time to be able to go home, have her dinner, compose herself, get some sleep. I think she was a bad sleeper always. So she took that time, but she was never late and never wasted any time. When she trusted people, she made no fuss. She never saw rushes, and I asked her why. "I have some idea, some notion of what I'm doing," she said, "and every time I see it, it falls so short that it throws me." She accomplished her work by intense concentration, relaxed concentration. She must have thought a great deal about the part beforehand, she had a clear image in her mind. On other films, they told me, she'd finish a scene and go straight to her dressing room. While we were shooting *Camille* on the back lot, she'd disappear to a little screened-off place and sunbathe. She didn't want to dissipate her energies. However, on the set she stayed around a good deal of the time on this picture and was very funny and sweet and, I think, fairly happy.

LAMBERT: It must have been a part she always wanted to play.

CUKOR: I think so, but she doesn't tell one about herself. She makes jokes, puts up a smokescreen, never really confides. She has beautiful manners and is a creature of the greatest distinction in bearing and every other way. There's a type of artist with something regal, to-the-manner-born in everything they do—I was reminded of her the other evening when I saw Nureyev taking his curtain calls. And, curiously enough, with the people she worked with, the crews and so on, she was very friendly. It wasn't an act. The conditions of working were important for her. And her bearing, her movement—if you remember, her movement is exceptional throughout the picture, it has its own *plastique*. She has that talent in a close-up to make the slightest gesture, the turn of her head, communicate something to you. And even when she's quiet, completely still, she conveys a sense of movement.

LAMBERT: Is it true that you shot two versions of the last scene, the death scene? In one she had a long speech and in the other practically no dialogue at all?

CUKOR: Yes, we did two versions, both beautifully played. But the screen is just too realistic for a long aria when someone's dying. It seemed unreal for a dying woman to talk so much. Another scene that was very tricky is when Armand's father comes to see her, and she agrees to give Armand up. It's when the conventions of the play show through most nakedly—but Garbo humanized it. And she did something on her own, you know, after the father left. She sank slowly to her knees and put her arms on the table. . . . She often did unexpected things. In the gambling casino scene, when she drops her fan and De Varville makes her pick it up, she made a remarkable movement, almost like something in a dance, like Isadora. She didn't kneel to pick it up, she bent sideways in the most beautiful way.

LAMBERT: Did she ever surprise you with one of these things during an actual take?

CUKOR: No, we'd discuss it, and I might suggest something, and she'd respond. She was very creative. When we shot the death scene, my mother had just died. I don't know exactly how much I conveyed my feelings about a dying woman to Garbo, but I seemed to recognize them in certain wonderful things she did, the way she used her voice, it was faded and gone. But she was always open and accessible to ideas. We were lucky, too, to have Robert Taylor. Armand's a notoriously bad part for an actor, and it's often played by men in their forties and doesn't make sense. But because Taylor was young it came alive.

LAMBERT: He had what Henry James called fresh credulity.

CUKOR: Exactly. The style of his speech was very American, and yet it didn't seem to matter too much. He rose to Garbo in those scenes when he denounced her, threw things at her. Taylor was a talented actor who became quite expert, but for a while he was frightened off by being called "beautiful Bob Taylor." In those days you had to be very virile or they thought you were degenerate. Now it can be hell for an actor to be good-looking.

LAMBERT: When we talked about *David Copperfield*, you said that you weren't happy with the art direction, but that in *Camille*—

CUKOR: Yes, I had some rough going on *David Copperfield*, but this time there was the greatest cooperation.

LAMBERT: The sets have a lightness that's uncharacteristic of other period movies of the time, which were usually more academic and solid.

CUKOR: The lightness is what I wanted.

LAMBERT: It's a period for which you obviously have great rapport.

CUKOR: I like that period—but period things have always fascinated me. They're in disrepute at the moment because they're expensive, and the actors often don't know how to play them, and they fall into overorating and all that. But then Fellini's *Satyricon* shows you just how wonderfully a period thing can be done now. I don't know whether Rome was remotely like that, but Fellini convinces me it was. After his film, I don't see how people can go back to the heavy architectural approach again.

LAMBERT: In *La Ronde*, Max Ophuls gave Anton Walbrook a line that was really about himself: "I adore the past." Is that also true of you?

CUKOR: One should be alive and have a sense of one's own time, but one should also have a sense of history. Quite often now I find an absolute ignorance and intolerance of the past.

LAMBERT: Doesn't the ignorance come from the intolerance, which comes from discontent with the present?

CUKOR: I suppose so, but if you know anything at all, you know the present's not that bad. I've been rereading George Moore's *Héloïse and Abélard*. University life seems very easy now compared to the violence in Europe in the Middle Ages. The students revolted with *total* violence then. It's a very interesting book—they had their troubadours, just like now, and they wandered around making a great deal of mischief. In fact, Héloïse's little son joined them and was never heard of again. He dropped out! So you see, it's never the end of the world. . . .

Interlude:
On D. W. Griffith

LAMBERT: When did you first meet Griffith?

CUKOR: It must have been in the middle or late thirties. He'd been out of work for some years and I thought it wicked that such a man should not be employed. (Later, I began to think the situation wasn't quite so simple.) I'd read the autobiography of the nineteenth-century actor Joseph Jefferson, which I drew on many years later for *Heller in Pink Tights*. Since Griffith had started as a young actor in touring shows, I told him about the book and he wrote a script called *The Moonlight Revellers*. The script is still in existence, I believe. Unfortunately, it wasn't very good, and instead of using his own personal experiences he fell back on too many theatrical clichés. Lilian Gish told me that before talkies Griffith never shot from a script. All those enormously complicated things stayed in his head, but because he was trained in the theater, he would rehearse long, long silent scenes. I find that difficult to imagine. Also, all his best pictures came out of his own experience—his feeling about the Civil War, and so on. He was a very mysterious man. He kept people at a distance all his life. He was charming, very distinguished, carried himself very well, but although it was difficult to tell much about him, I always had the impression he was unhappy. I liked him, but he wasn't easy. When the Screen Directors' Guild decided he would be the first one to receive a life membership, they organized this function and he was introduced from the stage, and all the famous directors present rose to their feet and applauded. Griffith stood and looked at them. Of course they were expecting something, but all he did was to say, "Oh, go to hell!" in a rather coy, silly way and sit down. He was trying to turn the whole thing into a joke, I suppose, but it seemed supremely tactless. We had the same lawyer, Lloyd Wright, who told me, "Griffith was a man of the greatest dignity. When he came into the room for a meeting at United Artists, his associates would rise to their feet." It was very tragic that his career stopped when he was still quite young.

LAMBERT: I imagine he was only about fifty when the talkies arrived.

CUKOR: About that, I think. Whether or not there was a physical deterioration, one can't be sure. He was so full of contradictions. He was very well read, you know, and yet he used those old theatrical melodramas for many of his best pictures, like *Broken Blossoms* and *Way Down East*, and made them into rather tragic and wonderful things. And I suppose he invented screen acting. . . . He was enormously prolific, of course. In the early days he made up pictures as he went along and shot a different picture every day. Perhaps he always wanted to do too much. He ran his own company, but I don't think he was a good businessman. And he spent himself producing other people's pictures.

LAMBERT: Although he was out of work for so many years, didn't he keep up with things? Wasn't he always very interested in what new directors were doing?

CUKOR: Yes, and he was always hoping to find a way back. Adolph Zukor tried to get him to go back, to work at Paramount, but nothing happened. Maybe he was incapable of it. I don't think he was a victim—I don't believe those stories of vendettas and people in the industry who wanted to punish him.

LAMBERT: Several of the greatest silent directors failed to make a successful transition to sound.

CUKOR: I know, but the curious thing is that Griffith came originally from the theater. You know, Artur Rubinstein once said that Adelina Patti refused to sing at rehearsals because, as she said, "There are just so many notes in the human voice," and she wouldn't spread herself. Rubinstein is convinced that the reason he plays so well at eighty is because he didn't work very hard when he was young. He points out that a pianist like Josef Hofmann, who studied and worked and practiced and played so much when he was very young, just burned himself out. But I don't think that's the whole story. There's the question of intelligence.

LAMBERT: And what happens in your life, and what it does to you.

CUKOR: What it does to you physically is important—your physical stamina, how much blood goes into the brain, how you look after yourself, all that.

LAMBERT: Griffith began drinking heavily in the twenties.

CUKOR: Very heavily, people said, though I never saw it myself. But it's the kiss of death, of course. It destroys people. Many people who drink heavily—and I think Griffith was one of them— are not reeling drunk, but their senses are dulled. They're too soaked to respond properly. I don't know exactly why Griffith began drinking, whether out of some personal unhappiness or because he saw his world beginning to float away. He loved the grand world and was very proud of having met people like Winston Churchill. The last years of his life were terribly sad, anyway. I'm afraid that drinkers end by alienating people, and they get terribly lonely. (*Astonished*) Imagine, dwindling away like that for almost twenty years after having practically invented silent pictures!

Holiday
(1938)
The Philadelphia Story
(1940)

LAMBERT: *Holiday* is one of my favorites. Like *The Philadelphia Story*, it's not only a very subtle, fluent adaptation of a play, it creates a genre all its own. Neither drama nor comedy, but something in between.

CUKOR: Phil Barry, who wrote both these plays, struck a particular note. His dialogue seemed to be realistic, but it wasn't really. The words always had a kind of rhythm underneath them, and the speech was sometimes quite elaborate. He required a particular kind of acting, too, lightly stylized but not affected. Both plays were originally directed in the theater by Arthur Hopkins, whom I admired enormously, as you know. (He also did another one by Barry, *In the Garden*, with Laurette Taylor, which I remember to this day.) I think Phil Barry's style—very witty, sometimes high-flown, sometimes sentimental—brought out a new kind of actress. Hope Williams, who did *Holiday* on the stage, had an elegance and gallantry that was all her own. Phil Barry had a rather "in" view of the rich, of the really grand people, and he wrote *Holiday* in the late twenties. It was quite a different thing to make fun of the rich at that time than when we made the movie ten years later, in the depths of the Depression.

LAMBERT: I hadn't realized it was a twenties play.

CUKOR: Yes, and they'd already made one sound film of it, with Ann Harding. And Kate Hepburn was Hope Williams' understudy on the stage. (The test that got her *A Bill of Divorcement* was a scene from the play. I remember how unslick it was. There was a moment when she had to pick up a drink, which was placed very inconveniently on the ground nearby. There was something very poignant in the way she made this difficult movement; her whole body moved me very much. Years later, when we finished shooting *Holiday*, she screened the original test at the company party. It looked very stagey and we laughed at it. But it had something. She reflected the rhythm of Phil Barry's lines by using a kind of singsong voice, which she used again at times in *The Philadelphia Story*.) Anyway, *Holiday* was a very happy picture to make.

LAMBERT: It looks very topical now. It's an outsider's view of the rich, because we see them through the eyes of the Cary Grant character, who falls in love with a rich girl but is really a thirties equivalent of the dropout. He prefers enjoying life to making money. There's a very telling scene when the girl's father, the head of the family, attacks "these new young ideas abroad in the world today," which he doesn't understand and condemns as "un-American."

CUKOR: You can imagine, when the play was originally written how that struck all the people making money hand over fist during the stock market boom. It was a good situation, this young man trying to explain to the girl that he wanted to enjoy life and then finding out from the way she reacted that she was the wrong girl for him. Phil Barry's comedies always had damn good situations, and like all good comedies the story was something that could have played seriously as well. I find it wonderful to take a serious subject and treat it with a kind of impertinence and gaiety. (If only this could be done with the situation of a black-and-white marriage today!) Phil Barry always skated on thin ice.

LAMBERT: He's very light, almost flip, then suddenly surprises you by turning serious. This happens all the way through *Holiday*. The rich girl finds Cary Grant's ideas rather amusing at first, but when she discovers he means business she's shocked and angry. Grant is almost patronizing toward her sister, the Katharine Hepburn part, then realizes she's the one for him. The two

Hepburn and Grant
rehearse a scene for
Holiday

Holiday: The butler
takes his hat and Cary
Grant enters the house
of the rich

sisters have pretended to like each other for years, but when the chips are down they dislike each other quite a lot.

CUKOR: And there's a very touching relationship between Lew Ayres, the drunken young brother, and Kate Hepburn.

LAMBERT: It's tough as well. I like it when he tells Hepburn, "You're wrong about your sister, she's not nearly as interesting as you think, she's really a very dull girl."

CUKOR: Barry had this gift for throwaway candor. There's a lot of what Fanny Brice used to call meat and potatoes.

LAMBERT: I never saw either play on the stage, but I'm sure the movies improve on both of them. It's a style, that "throwaway candor," which seems perfect for the intimacy of the screen.

CUKOR: The trick is not to play it "all out." It's a question of subtle, understated attitudes. Some artificial comedy is very hard to do on the screen because you play from point to point. On the stage you can play for laughs and wait for them. On the screen you have to get the laughs without playing for them. When we did *Born Yesterday*, Judy Holliday had already played it for two years on the stage. We'd rehearse on the set, the crew would laugh, it looked all right—then when we shot it she had to play the same thing to total silence, and it disconcerted her at first.

LAMBERT: Both films have many funny moments but hardly any belly laughs. The tone of the comedy is very delicate, nothing ostentatious about it.

CUKOR: As Phil Barry showed, there's nothing ostentatious about the rich way of life. They have these great houses but they don't seem to display them. Everything's played down. The sisters in *Holiday* are rivals, but they're never bitchy about it. The breeding determines the kind of comedy.

LAMBERT: And from time to time there's a rueful note. At first you think Hepburn is just a poor little rich girl out of sympathy with her father's values. Then you find out the self-pity in the character. She enjoys dramatizing her situation, being sensitive and misunderstood.

CUKOR: Yes, she doesn't quite have the courage to chuck it all, which is why she falls for the man who does. It's all very skillfully worked out.

LAMBERT: Both you and Barry love to deal in nuances. Maybe that's why his material suited you so well.

CUKOR: He was a subtle writer, but nothing muddy about him. A clarity at the back of it all. I don't like muddiness, I like clarity. It has nothing to do with being literal, and it doesn't cut out mystery—of course, there are times when you don't want to say everything—but I like to know that I can look into the pool of water when I want to and find it clear at the bottom.

LAMBERT: And in *Holiday* you can. Nobody at first is quite what he seems; all the characters react surprisingly. When she realizes that Grant is going to walk out on her, the rich girl is suddenly very happy. She says, "I'm so relieved, I could sing!" That's the charm of Barry's writing. And you handle it with a tremendous *ease*, which is what makes *Holiday* so appealing.

CUKOR: When M-G-M bought the rights to *The Philadelphia Story*, they made a recording of a stage performance of the play. The idea was to find out where the laughs came. After the picture was made, we checked it against the recording and the laughs came quite differently. In the theater all the comedy was in Phil Barry's verbal wit, but in the movie a lot of it was visual, reactions, pieces of business, and so on. That's why I believe in letting comedy *happen* on the screen. When people complain about audience laughter drowning out a funny moment in a movie, I tell them, "Well, you can always go and see it again." It's a very pleasing complaint. The alternative is to go for something mechanical, and you can see the dire results of canned laughter on TV. The actors know the value of the comedy, but they have to let it out in a fresh, apparently improvised way. Kate Hepburn had done *The Philadelphia Story* on the stage, and there were a couple of scenes with serious overtones in which she wept. I suggested that for the movie she didn't weep. She was doubtful at first, then she tried—and it came out much fresher.

LAMBERT: Was anyone except Hepburn in the play and the film?

CUKOR: No. Kate had part ownership of the play, and there was a stipulation in the movie deal that she had to be in it, too. In so many cases like this they cast somebody else. I believe at this time she was considered box-office poison, and she very shrewdly had it in her contract that the two leading men should be big stars. We tried to get this and that star, but they weren't available, and we finally chose Cary Grant and James Stewart, neither of whom was considered absolutely top-notch at the time—and they were perfect.

LAMBERT: Why do you think Hepburn was labeled box-office poison?

CUKOR: She was never a "love me, I'm a lovable little girl" kind of actress. She always challenged the audience, and that wasn't the fashion in those days. On the hoof, when people first saw her, they felt something arrogant in her playing. Later, by sheer feeling and skill, she bent them to her will. Of course, her quality of not asking for pity, not caring whether people liked her or not, was ideal for *The Philadelphia Story*. Barry wrote it for her.

LAMBERT: In this play, more openly than in *Holiday*, Barry really seems to think the rich are the most marvelous people on earth.

CUKOR (*amused*): Maybe so do I. Let's face it—don't *you*?

LAMBERT: Only some of them.

CUKOR: Well, I find them a great comfort.

LAMBERT: Reassuring?

CUKOR: Very.

LAMBERT: Barry almost starts to make a judgment on the rich in *The Philadelphia Story*, then he draws back and finds them totally charming and glamorous after all.

CUKOR: Yes, he starts to put them down but ends up very cozy with them. Of course, it was different at that time. The rich were pleased to be rich. Now they're hangdog about it. I try and reassure my rich friends, "Oh, everybody's really mad about you!" But they move into smaller houses all the same and don't want to be singled out. Elizabeth Taylor is the last of the great splurgers.

LAMBERT: In 1940 those rich families hadn't become "democratic." They were defiantly exclusive; they shut themselves up in a kind of fortress world.

CUKOR: Maybe in self-defense. I think they already had an inkling of the tumbrels. . . . Barry's stage directions, by the way, were very clever. In describing the house, he wrote, "The place is very grand but by no means a palace. There are economical touches, like rattan furniture with homemade slipcovers. They give an impression of grandeur more by their self-possession, the way they assume their exclusivity." He really knew the rich.

LAMBERT: That description is very well reflected in your sets. Their luxury is very unobtrusive.

CUKOR: Understated, yes, but did you notice the footmen and butlers? Masses of them, all perfectly self-possessed!

LAMBERT: A typical touch. The pace of the film is quite leisurely for a comedy, by the way. It takes its time and builds up detail. And it ends by giving you a real portrait of these people and their life at that time.

CUKOR: The material determined the tempo. You couldn't take it too quickly, because these are people for whom conversation is a kind of art, they say witty things and they're witty about serious things. You couldn't play it as if it were situation comedy. There *was* a situation, of course, and you had to be very careful about that, too, and make sure it never got hokey-pokey. What is funny

The Philadelphia Story: James Stewart to Katharine Hepburn,
"You are the golden girl . . ."

about Kate's performance is her dilemma. She believes herself in love with three different men at the same time, and she behaves as if it's the most important situation in the world. She told me that when she did the play, she was very startled by the audience reaction on opening night in New Haven. She herself found the situation in the third act quite moving and tragic, but people began laughing. It got worse and worse, she became furious. She had to make a quick exit, and she muttered to someone in the wings, "They hate it, they hate it!" Much to her astonishment, everyone backstage was grinning with delight.

LAMBERT: The comedy of the situation is that only *she* thinks it's tragic.

CUKOR: And the play is really a fairy tale with a moral about humility. She meets her prince but gums it up and has to rediscover him and herself all over again. It's one of the few comedies with real suspense, you know, because up to the last moment you're not sure who she's going to marry.

LAMBERT: *Holiday* and *The Philadelphia Story* have a lot of dialogue, but they never seem stagebound. The way you put the same wine in a new bottle is masterly.

CUKOR: The first thing in transferring plays to the screen is not to discombobulate the original, you mustn't tear it apart. On the other hand, you can't just film the actors speaking their lines. You have to find a new *movement* for the screen, and that starts in the writing. Donald Ogden Stewart, who was a friend of Phil Barry's, adapted *The Philadelphia Story* with the greatest modesty and unselfishness. He wrote in a couple of original scenes, but very much in the manner of Barry. He served the thing, he didn't try to star himself, and yet people realized what a subtle piece of work he'd done, because he won the Oscar for the best screen adaptation that year.

LAMBERT: The prologue's a good example of that. It sums up the way the marriage between Hepburn and Grant ended without a word. He walks out of the house carrying a bag of golf clubs. Hepburn appears in the doorway carrying a club he's forgotten. Instead of giving it to him, she breaks it in two. Grant looks furious, then does this marvelous thing of advancing on her as if he's going to hit her—then simply gives her a contemptuous push, sending her into a pratfall.

CUKOR: You know, we shot that as an afterthought! We realized we needed something to reconstruct their marriage, and we didn't want to do it with a lot of dialogue. Also, you understand Kate's fury when Cary Grant turns up again on the eve of her new marriage. It's a movie scene that doesn't violate the original structure, just as the actors add something new by approaching the same situations in a different way. That's the secret, I think.

Interlude:
On Television, Mr. Hitchcock
and Funerals

CUKOR: We're really very ungrateful to television. I never watch a series or anything like that, of course, but I watch it in the morning and while I'm brushing my teeth at night, and all kinds of unexpected goodies happen. The other night I saw a newsreel of Prince Charles performing at Oxford. He came out and did some skits, rather badly but with enormous charm. He pretended to be a Scots bagpipe player, then he became an octopus and rolled around on the floor. Isn't that the greatest thing that ever happened to royalty? And where else could you find out about it?

LAMBERT: Television for you seems rather like the *Times* of London for Mr. Hitchcock. He says it's the only newspaper he reads to keep in touch with what's going on because he finds its rather peculiar outlook on the world terribly stimulating.

CUKOR (*highly amused*): Oh, he's so perverse! He'd never tell you what he really thinks, never, never! I have the greatest respect and admiration for him, but he will *never* tell you! He's absolutely impassive and says ridiculous things in this solemn

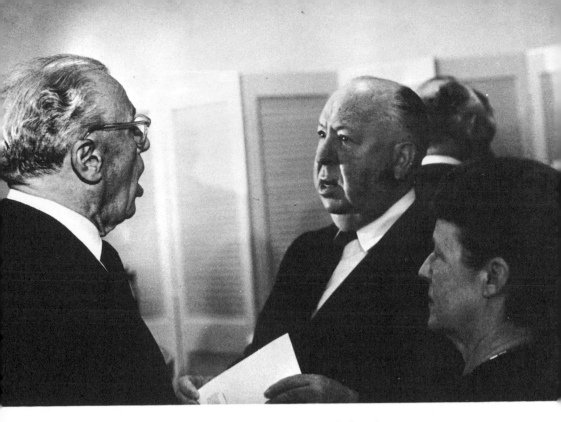

Cukor meets Hitchcock, with Mrs. Hitchcock

way. Extraordinarily enough, he's a very religious man. Would you know that?

LAMBERT: No.

CUKOR: But he is. He's always going to church. It's marvelous!

LAMBERT: When the *Cahiers du Cinéma* critics started the great Hitchcock revival a few years ago, they fastened onto his Catholic upbringing and the Catholic element in his work. But when they asked him about it in interviews, he was evasive about it.

CUKOR: It doesn't seem to jibe with him at all.

LAMBERT: There's something wonderfully devious about intelligent Catholics. Doesn't that jibe?

CUKOR (*rather perplexed*): And he's fascinated by all kinds of ignoble things. I don't understand that either.

LAMBERT: A lot of Catholic writers—Graham Greene, Mauriac —are fascinated by the ignoble, too.

CUKOR: Well, I have my own kind of religion, which is going to funerals. So many of my friends have died. (As Noel Coward said,

"If your friends just last through lunch. . . .") For one whole year, Kate Hepburn and I—she's a funeral girl, *very* conscientious —went to a funeral every Saturday. She had a special funeral costume. We'd listen to all the prayers, and I'd think, "Isn't it wonderful you people really believe all this, you think you're off to Heaven or wherever, isn't it wonderful?" But the Catholic funerals are more tricky. There's a moment when you have to sink your knees in front of the altar, but the *fine* point is you must lower your head very respectfully *before* you sink to your knees. It takes real timing, and you can easily miss your cue, unless you watch other people.

LAMBERT: Do you object to the showbiz element of funerals here?

CUKOR: No. I realize the comedy of Forest Lawn, but if it's a comfort to the bereaved, why not? And it's all so pretty. All the statues and the places with marvelous names, the columbarium of prayer and all that. . . . David Selznick and I used to laugh at one of the mortuary ads that boasted about the quality of its earth. (*Almost convulsed, suddenly*) "Warm, dry soil—no seepage!"

Zaza
(1938)

LAMBERT: You are smiling before I've said a word this morning because you know I screened *Zaza* yesterday and I liked it. (*Cukor's smile continues, almost stop-frame.*) Really! In spite of all the censorship cuts—

CUKOR (*the smile vanishes*): But what was *left?* It was a story of adultery, and after we finished the picture it got an absolute turndown by the Hays office! The whole basic plot is that a married man has an affair with a music-hall singer, there are these long despairing scenes, and they're all CUT!

LAMBERT: They have one love scene before she discovers he's married. Everything between them after that, I suppose, is gone?

CUKOR: Everything!

LAMBERT: But there's still eighty minutes or so of really elegant moviemaking.

CUKOR (*relenting a little*): I won't be sentimental about something that was a failure and did so badly at the box office—and with a situation that most people today would find comic—but I

Claudette Colbert and Bert Lahr in a music-hall scene from *Zaza*

Helen Westley in *Zaza*

On the set of *Zaza*: Cukor with Fanny Brice, who coached Colbert in the music-hall scenes

know the *look* of it. There was a man at Paramount then called Hans Dreier, and he did very atmospheric sets.

LAMBERT: The period feeling of *Zaza* is just as good as in *Camille*. Quite different from most American costume movies set in Europe.

CUKOR (*warming up*): I came up against less resistance at Paramount than at Metro. As I remember it, *Zaza* seemed to go awfully easy there. The sets had taste, we reconstructed that outdoor theater—

LAMBERT: Visually the picture holds your interest, even if the remains of the story don't. But Herbert Marshall is so stuffy as the lover, I'm glad they cut some of his scenes.

CUKOR: He was considered very attractive at the time. Audiences liked him. But I agree he wasn't right—very English and tired.

LAMBERT: The feeling of a French touring music-hall company reminds me of Colette. In *The Vagabond* she describes how impossible it was to have any privacy. This is very well done in *Zaza*;

the whole company knows about her affair and discusses it openly.

CUKOR: Yes, it has that kind of atmosphere. And it was the only time that Claudette Colbert, who has a very pretty voice, ever sang in a picture. Fanny Brice, a great friend of mine, came and coached her. (I'm a great believer in that kind of thing. For the "Belle Hélène" scenes in *Heller in Pink Tights* I got Fritzi Massary to help Sophia Loren.) I remember Fanny Brice telling Claudette how to contact an audience. It was really the distilled knowledge of a lifetime. Fanny was a very intelligent woman who retained her ordinary Brooklyn speech even when she became very elegant and sophisticated. She told Claudette, "You know, kid, when you sing a ballad you'll find it a comfort to touch your own flesh." And she placed her hand around the base of her throat. She had very beautiful hands. "When you sing a ballad, if you touch your own flesh, it's a kind of comfort to ya." Fanny had discovered the Delsarte method, which teaches body love, all on her own. Claudette had to come out in front of the curtains of a stage and begin a song, and Fanny showed her how to get an audience's attention. She had this radiant smile, and although she never looked directly at anyone in the audience, she made everyone feel "she's looking at *me*." "When they calm down," she'd say, "especially if it's a serious song, I fasten my eyes right on the balcony, right below the balcony, kid, and I sing." All this was really invaluable.

LAMBERT: And comes across. You not only believe Colbert as a successful singer, but she shows a side of herself I've never seen in any other picture. She was always highly accomplished, but in *Zaza* there's something much more personal.

CUKOR: I'm happy to hear that. Claudette started on the stage and then became this very skillful comedienne in pictures, but she used only part of her great talent. She had a much bigger range than she chose to show.

LAMBERT: She really exposes herself. There's a surprising depth to her.

CUKOR: It didn't surprise me because I always knew she had it.

LAMBERT: Perhaps it's easier to respond to *Zaza* now. A lot of recent movies have conditioned us to react to atmosphere rather than plot. One knows *Zaza* has been cut, feels the cuts, doesn't care about Herbert Marshall—and is left free to appreciate all the other qualities, Colbert's performance, the humor and the elegance. It's very effortless, by the way, and never self-consciously "frenchy."

CUKOR: Yes, it had a real look. The outdoor cabaret was good; we even had real earth on the ground. And the picture was wonderfully photographed by Charles Lang, who's still going strong.

LAMBERT: There's one stunning shot of Colbert in her bedroom. She's lying on the bed, an old brass bedstead, and the lighting is very muted and blurry; all the objects in the room stand out very solidly, like an interior by Bonnard.

CUKOR: Lang could always make the women look ravishing and the sets seem right. I'm really beginning to feel sorry the picture didn't go. It was terribly French, of course, that endless exploration of unfaithfulness and the suffering of love. . . . But you've quite set me up for the day!

The Women
(1939)
The Chapman Report
(1962)

CUKOR: For starters, *The Women* had a very weak and foolish central story, a kind of obligatory story—"prepostrious," as Ethel Barrymore used to say. It just didn't fit with the rest.

LAMBERT: It was the same thing in the play.

CUKOR: But maybe we sentimentalized it more in the movie. At the time it probably wasn't as silly as it seems now, because it came from a different world. "Kept women" and marital breakups were big moral questions then. Now, of course, everybody would be screwing everybody, and everybody would know about it.

LAMBERT: All the women would be doing much wilder things.

CUKOR: Yes, Crystal wouldn't be a kept woman, she'd be carrying on with another girl. Billie Burke said about the picture, "It's like a *Merry Wives of Windsor*, when some women set the whole city on its ears." It's a big hoop-de-doo, a circus, and in a sense you had to be a lion tamer with all those ladies. . . . I thought Rosalind Russell was very good—it was her first comedy part and she'd never had an audience really like her as a straight leading lady. So she really grabbed hold of the part and didn't worry about not being sympathetic.

LAMBERT: She is definitely ruthless.

CUKOR: Ruthless *and* comic, which is important. It was broad low comedy, but it was also true. You felt this in the scene when she went to Reno to get her divorce and had this sudden tantrum, the tantrum of a naughty eleven-year-old girl who'd never been properly slapped. It was very original, the way she played that scene. (*A grimace*) But didn't you think the clothes were perfectly dreadful? Adrian was trying to knock them dead.

LAMBERT: Yes, I was surprised how tacky they looked.

CUKOR: A tacky period, the early forties, mind you—all those very fancy hairdos and broad shoulders. I think Adrian was trying too hard. And the scene of the fashion show—

LAMBERT: It has nothing to do with anything else. I imagine the front office imposed it?

CUKOR: Yes, they just wanted us to put in a fashion show. I went to a show here and I realized the nuances of a thing like that are very difficult to do. Designers have to create something sensational to catch the eye, but that's not the real work, and the real work isn't photographable—it's a question of the total effect, the idea behind the show. All we had were some very bad and flashy clothes. Like the serious parts of the picture, they were no good.

LAMBERT: The idea of setting off all the monstrous comic creatures against one ordinary, rather nice lady is all right in itself. But the ordinary lady didn't have to be such a bore. She should have been more foolish, more helpless. She would certainly have lost out in the end. Instead of which, you feel she's there to send the audience home happy, to make them feel a nice, dim woman can always keep her husband.

CUKOR (*a sigh*): So worthy and self-righteous! And with *nobility* on her side!

LAMBERT: There's a point of view on all the comic characters—they're satirized. But no point of view at all on the nice woman.

CUKOR: Alas, that happens very often with a straight character.

LAMBERT: But a lot of the comedy survives. I particularly like the opening ten minutes—those short, impressionistic scenes that introduce all the ladies going about their horrific business, fast and crisp and beautifully timed. The pacing of the comedy dialogue is quite unique. In many other comedies of that period, like *His Girl Friday*, you feel the pace is just an end in itself, a technical thing, the actors are made to fire off their cracks as quickly as possible. Here the pace seems to come from the characters themselves. They rattle out the lines and interrupt and overlap each other, and it's because they're so frantic and urgent about just *being* bitches.

CUKOR: Really? Well, that's very good.

LAMBERT: None of the comic ladies seems to mind how awful she is. They don't compromise, and that's why the comedy doesn't date.

CUKOR: I think they were all on a horror kick. Anita Loos wrote some very lively new scenes for the picture. You remember when a lot of the women go into a little ladies' room at the same time? It was played as quickly as any human beings can play anything. They were gossiping about their hostess and they had to sandwich all the details very quickly. Then, right in the middle, one of them picked up a hand towel and said, "What cheap Chinese embroidery!"

LAMBERT: And another comments on the soap, "Only ten cents a bar!"

CUKOR: All in the middle of this intense gossip. And then there were some nuances of speech I thought rather witty. (Some, I may say, were my suggestions.) Rosalind Russell was very broad and tough, but when she used a French expression she spoke it perfectly, and you knew she'd been to one of those schools in Switzerland. It was original, too, only to show women in the whole picture. No shot of a man anywhere. I believe in the remake they brought in men.

LAMBERT: I believe so. The satire is quite reminiscent of *Dinner at Eight*; there's a desperation underlying the comedy.

CUKOR: Well, did you know that George Kaufman, who wrote *Dinner at Eight*, helped on the play of *The Women*? Clare Boothe Luce wrote it, of course, but he was brought in to guide the rewrite out of town.

LAMBERT: There's one sentimental scene, however, that really comes off—when the girl played by Joan Fontaine reconciles with her husband on the telephone.

CUKOR: Joan was a very pretty girl, and I believe I'd made a test of her, I had her read for *Gone with the Wind*. I'd always remembered her. She had a not very successful career as a leading

A fight on the divorce ranch. Norma Shearer, Rosalind Russell, Joan Fontaine, Paulette Goddard and Mary Boland in *The Women*

lady at RKO, and she was free at this time. I told the studio they ought to take an option on her, but they didn't. Anyway, it was an interesting moment when she played her scene on the telephone. Up to then she'd wanted to be an actress but was never really sure she could act. Now she felt a power, and as a result of this scene, the experience it gave her, she felt, "Yes, I was right to try, I can act. . . ." I think it had a great deal to do with her getting the part in *Rebecca*. . . . But I'm glad you found the comedy still funny. So often comedy doesn't stand up, it dates very quickly. Certain things are in the air at the time, then you become detached from them. One never knows. In a few years' time, I should think all the worship of motorcycle riders will seem—

LAMBERT: Totally nostalgic?

CUKOR: Or a great bore.

LAMBERT: Both *The Women* and *The Chapman Report*, which you made more than twenty years later, deal with the lives of fairly well-to-do but discontented ladies—

CUKOR: Except that *The Women's* New York, and in *The Chapman Report* they're suburban. The New York women were a cut higher, they'd lunch at the Colony. These are more bourgeois.

LAMBERT: And the problems have certainly changed. *The Women* had very tame things to deal with—a husband having an affair with a shopgirl, and so on. In the sixties the world looks much darker. You have your nymphomania, frigidity, father complexes—

CUKOR: But *now* it's gone so much further, the problems would be different again. I don't know what they would be now?

LAMBERT: Yes, you do. Lesbians, men-swapping—

CUKOR: Yes, yes, yes, all of that!

LAMBERT: Did any contrast between the two pictures occur to you when you made *The Chapman Report*?

CUKOR: Not at all. It was years later and it never occurred to me. The novel of *The Chapman Report*, although it was written rather sensationally, seemed to me to have its points. It presented something contemporary (at the time) about outwardly respectable women who were frigid and took lovers and went to psychiatrists.

LAMBERT: Your movie, anyway, was a serious attempt to crack the façade of this kind of respectability.

CUKOR: But it was cut in a cruel way! We had a preview in San Francisco and it went extremely well—in fact, I thought the audience was ahead of it and wanted more rather than less. But the censors had come in already, and those were the days when we didn't fight them. It was emasculated.

LAMBERT: Was it Darryl Zanuck who did the cutting?

CUKOR: It was cut for the censors first, then Zanuck cut it again. He hadn't come to the preview, but he started to "fix it up." Now, what was really first class in the picture were those long, sustained interviews with the women who confide their problems to the psychiatrist making this report. They can't see him, he talks to them from behind a screen. The scenes were extremely well played: Jane Fonda had an emotional one that was particularly good—

LAMBERT: And beautifully conceived. A very dramatic use of color and composition. She wears this too-girlish white dress, a big white hat shielding half her face, and this nervous, frigid figure in white is very striking against the neutral tones of the office and the darkness of the screen—

CUKOR: But it was all cut, cut, CUT! She had many big scenes that were cut.

LAMBERT: Didn't you want those scenes played entirely on the actresses? Never cutting away to the psychiatrist behind the screen?

CUKOR: I cut to him very occasionally, very briefly. Most of those sustained scenes were played directly on the actresses, but in the final cut they were all chopped up and made to seem backwards-and-forwards in the usual manner. And Claire Bloom's most important scene, the gang rape, was chopped to bits. It was a scene of really extraordinary power. I know one always talks this way when a picture doesn't turn out, but in this case it was *definitely* so! Everything original in the picture was really hurt. The end, which had a kind of ordinary melodrama, was the only thing they didn't touch.

When you undertake to do anything, you should know why. What is the point of doing it? The point here was a rather freshly written insight into the sexual problems of "respectable" women at that time. Most of this insight was cut.

With Anita Loos on the set of *The Women*

LAMBERT: The cutting also shows up in various plot points that aren't followed through, particularly in the episodes with Claire Bloom. Her character is fragmented, though you can still see a remarkable performance.

CUKOR: I thought the nymphomaniac should not be at all obvious or common—really a lady, and really very nice. That gave it something poignant. I knew someone like that, adorable and distinguished but messed up. Claire had some long, sustained scenes, too, and they were cut. She played them without interruption and with great range. She's a mysterious girl in real life, very sweet, but one never knows what she's like. She'd played many classical parts in the theater, and I remember at the end, when she took the sleeping pills, I suggested it might be a little like Juliet taking the potion.

LAMBERT: She moved with a kind of hopelessness and looseness that told a great deal about the character.

CUKOR: Yes, the skill was dazzling. I kept on seeing this woman I knew. . . . And the clothes by Orry-Kelly were very original. Each woman wore a single color all the way through: Jane always wore white, Claire was always in black, Glynis Johns in beige. Claire wore no bra, so her breasts moved, and it seemed very erotic, you always felt the dress was going to fall off or one of her breasts would pop out. And she did all those ignoble things with a beautiful, somber face. . . .

[142]

The Chapman Report:
Jane Fonda

Directing Claire Bloom in
The Chapman Report

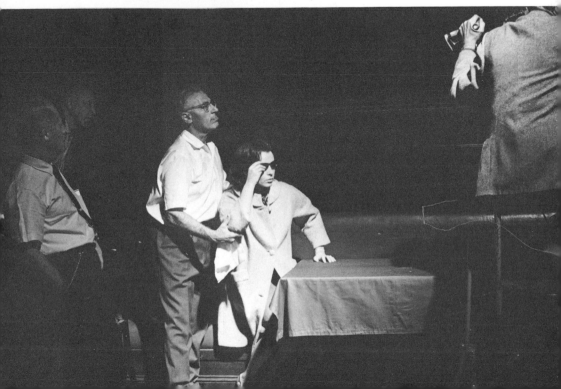

LAMBERT: If they hadn't given into the censors, if Zanuck could have been kept away from it, the picture might have been very successful. In some ways—its approach to sexual things—it was a bit ahead of its time.

CUKOR: And without vulgarity. But there was a political situation, too. Zanuck's son produced the picture for Fox but Warners released it. We had two front offices, the short end of the stick in every way. And it's too bad. The picture did have some virtues. I've seen that happen very often: A picture fails, but even in its failure are some of the best things I've been involved with. But it gets nowhere in the end and grosses nothing, because the story doesn't carry you.

LAMBERT: The picture joins *Zaza* and *Bhowani Junction* and *A Star Is Born* as examples of your work seriously damaged by cutting.

Interlude:
On Vivien Leigh

CUKOR: First of all, Vivien was a really wonderful screen actress. Quite apart from her looks she had something very strong and individual and interesting. I also saw her act very well on the stage. She was brilliant as Shaw's Cleopatra, and she made a damn good stab at Lady Macbeth.

LAMBERT: A much underrated performance.

CUKOR: She was often underrated because she was so beautiful.

LAMBERT: And many of the London theater critics seemed to bear a grudge against her. There was always the implication that Olivier was "carrying" her.

CUKOR: Absolutely untrue. She did remarkable things on her own, in *Duel of Angels*, a very difficult part. And I wish I'd seen her in *Lady of the Camellias*. She said it was the part she liked best. She was a consummate actress anyway, hampered by beauty —and as a person the complete romantic. She had this great talent for creating beauty around her, she made exquisite gardens, she

A New Year's Eve party (1940)
at David Selznick's house:
celebrants include (left to right)
Vivien Leigh, Laurence Olivier,
Selznick, Cukor, Irene Selznick,
Merle Oberon

dressed ravishingly, she had true breeding, and when she invited you to dinner, the food and everything were perfect.

LAMBERT: She sometimes gave me the impression that this desire for beauty and order around her was to compensate for a disorder under the surface.

CUKOR: Yes, you felt something tragic even when she was at her happiest. Somehow, I wasn't surprised when I heard she'd died. And Kate Hepburn said at once, "Oh, thank God!" because she'd suffered so much and was so miserable, really, from the time her marriage with Olivier broke up to the end of her life. Although most of the time you'd never suspect it. She was Rabelaisian, this exquisite creature, and told outrageous jokes in that voice cool and pretty enough to make you weep. I remember taking her to see Cole Porter not long before he died. He'd had a leg amputated and was wretched and didn't see many people, but he wanted to see Vivien. He couldn't move, he could only lie there, and it was painful, but Vivien was so entertaining and he obviously loved her being there. She'd dressed very stunningly and covered her fingers with rings, like a gypsy fortune-teller. I'd never seen that before, though it's very fashionable now. From time to time we had to leave the room when a nurse had to give Cole Porter a shot of something. Then we'd come back, and Vivien never let up, and he was entranced. When we left and got into the car, she chose to sit up front, next to the driver. She was silent for a long time. Then she turned around, and I saw she'd been weeping, her eyes were filled with tears.

LAMBERT: That's wildly romantic and so like her.

CUKOR: As a friend she was always very tender and appreciative. I remember a big party I gave for her the first time she was out here after her separation from Larry. It was the full Hollywood thing with fountains and bands and a swimming pool. She came in, looking absolutely beautiful, and said at once, "Ooh, darling, can you really afford this?" Then, as it was a Sunday night and she knew I was working next day, she came over at a certain time and said, "Let me tell them all to fuck off now!"

LAMBERT: She once told me that you'd absolutely laid out for her the part of Scarlett O'Hara in the tests and rehearsals and talks. Having seen the tests, I know exactly what she means. It was another instantaneous meeting of the actress and the part.

CUKOR: There's a funny story that Olivia de Havilland tells

about this. After I left the picture, Olivia would come over to my house and do some moonlighting with me—I'd run the scenes with her, and so on. She felt rather guilty about going behind Vivien's back, until she found out that Vivien was doing exactly the same thing, too. And did you know that Vivien and Olivia, when they heard I'd been removed from the picture, were both dressed in their widows' garb that day? They rushed over to David Selznick's office, all in black, and pleaded and threatened and did everything in the world, but he remained obdurate. I was rather touched when I heard about that.

LAMBERT: In the tests you shot Vivien hadn't mastered her Southern accent, but everything else had complete grasp and authority. And one scene, when she's trying to get Ashley back after the war, she plays even better than in the finished film. It had a kind of neurotic power, really desperate and frightening. Victor Fleming's version seems almost tame in comparison.

CUKOR: Yes, that was much better in the test, and Vivien knew it. At that time they still shot six days a week, and the picture was going on and on, and she wanted to get back to Larry, who was in England. She was exhausted and impatient and would come and spend every Sunday here. One day she arrived, took a swim, lay down on a sofa in the sun and fell into deep, absolute sleep. She was out for several hours, then she woke up, giggled and told me, "I was an awful bitch on the set yesterday." They'd been trying that very scene with Ashley, and she felt it wasn't right, so she made poor Victor Fleming trot over and screen the test. That was so typically straight-shooting of her, as an actress and a human being.

Susan and God
(1940)

LAMBERT: *Susan and God* has been overshadowed by the two films you made before and after—*The Women*, which is more obstreperous, and *The Philadelphia Story*, which is more high style. But the first half has some lively satire—and a nice portrait of a silly, frivolous woman who latches onto Moral Rearmament, the Billy Grahamism of the time, and nearly destroys several lives in doing so. It was quite a daring subject to take on at the time, I suppose?

CUKOR: Yes, the studio took a chance in making it, in a way, but then the big companies often took more chances than they're credited with. We started with the advantage that *Susan and God* had been a very successful Broadway play, of course—written by Rachel Crothers and starring Gertie Lawrence. I didn't see it on the stage. As a rule, when a thing is playing on the stage, I don't mind borrowing. I don't believe in saying, "I never saw it so I couldn't have copied it." I didn't *happen* to have seen this one, but normally I take a look, and if there's anything good I damn well take *that*, too.

LAMBERT: Joan Crawford comes out of it as a real performer.

CUKOR: Yes, she lent herself to it and really played a character.

LAMBERT: In the second half, when the story turns sentimental, she starts to go back and conform to her old movie star image, but up to that time she's really very accomplished and funny.

CUKOR: Well, I must take the blame for some of that, if there's blame to be attached. She should have remained a foolish woman all the way through, even when she was coming to her senses. I should have talked to her, we should have understood together. . . . So put a black mark against me.

LAMBERT: Did she *want* to act?

CUKOR: Oh, she was excited by it! We did *A Woman's Face* later, where she played a serious character part. And when she went on to do *Mildred Pierce* later and won an Academy Award, I thought our two films might have had something to do with it.

LAMBERT: You once said that the bad side of the star system was that it encouraged stars to trade on their personalities rather than work at the real business of acting.

CUKOR: The star system is the cult of personality. It may be a personality rather than a talent that catches the eye and the attention in the first place. Then, if it doesn't develop, it grows threadbare. And these people were not always encouraged to develop, to change. Thalberg was one of the few who really tried to make his stars do surprising things, try different kinds of parts.

LAMBERT: Rita Hayworth also has a small part in the picture. Wasn't it the beginning of her escape from the B's?

CUKOR: Yes, she'd read for me for *Holiday*—the part of Kate's sister—a couple of years before, at Columbia, where she was under contract. She was too young for that part, but I thought her attractive and gifted. I remembered her and borrowed her for Metro for *Susan and God*.

LAMBERT: There's one moment—at the party, when she starts to rumba—and the Rita Hayworth of the future is all there.

CUKOR: Yes, I think it helped her to really get started. There were some other young girls in small parts, too. A gifted girl, Susan Peters, who had a tragic accident—

LAMBERT: Yes, at the Moral Rearmament jamboree—a very good scene, almost spookily topical, with its earnest, self-righteous, Billy Grahamish feeling—you can spot, among the kids looking very patriotic in the background, Susan Peters, Joan Leslie and Gloria de Haven. And the journalist is Dan Dailey.

CUKOR: He'd just come out here. Very good, wasn't he?

LAMBERT: He looked marvelously disgusted when they sang the inspirational song.

CUKOR: It's fun, going back through one's work and spotting these people and saying, "Ah, they're rather good. . . ." I have a hunch about acting ability, you know. And it's a matter of luck, too. (*Thoughtful*) Yes—hunch, luck and a nose for it!

LAMBERT: The very characteristic thing about the comedy in the picture is how you never take sides. You don't encourage the audience to think Moral Rearmament is absurd, nor do you lead them on to believe in it. You just tell them to watch and see what happens to this particular woman.

CUKOR: I believe in the detached approach for comedy. If you *really look* at anything, there's always a comic note. A painful note, too. One brings the other to life. And sometimes you establish the most immediate connections with the lightest of touches. I know that's not considered very serious in some quarters. They think it's frivolous.

LAMBERT: Only if they equate worthiness with seriousness. . . . *Susan and God* is a minor comedy, like *Her Cardboard Lover,* very professional rather than personal—but Crawford's performance is still very apt. That kind of woman is still around. Well-to-do and empty. She goes in for one of the self-realization cults now, or group therapy in the nude.

LAMBERT: You believe in the detached approach for comedy. Is that one reason you like Andy Warhol's films so much?

CUKOR: Yes. He makes a marvelous kind of world, and a marvelous kind of mischief, holding nothing back and just watching it happen. I applaud him for doing that most difficult thing, combining semipornography and comedy. (*Pause*) No, not semipornography. His films are not sexually arousing. He collects grotesqueries, like Mr. Fellini. And some of them happen to be sexual grotesqueries.

Susan and God:
Joan Crawford
tries to convert
Ruth Hussey
and Bruce
Cabot

LAMBERT: He holds nothing back because he doesn't take sides. There's no comment implied—and it frees his people. They find themselves in a climate where they can go all the way.

CUKOR: "Personal expression" is a much abused expression, but these films are a real personal expression of Andy Warhol and Paul Morrissey. Nobody else has done anything like it. The selection of people, the casting, is absolutely brilliant and imperti-

Emergence of
Rita Hayworth:
with Bruce
Cabot and Rose
Hobart in *Susan
and God*

nent. The life they see, the gutter they see, or the world they see, is so funny and agonizing, and they see it so vividly, with such humor. I've never seen any documentaries or any "low life" studies that have a grain of humor. They're usually soggy, or they have that deadly touch of the schoolmaster.

LAMBERT: Or they're trying deliberately to shock you.

CUKOR: Yes, or they have that completely impersonal, inartistic approach—setting up a camera in a bar or whatever and grabbing what they can. But to present this picture of a world, to do it with such original humor—I'm lost in admiration. I adored *Lonesome Cowboys*. And *Flesh*. And *Trash*.

LAMBERT: Of course, Morrissey dramatizes things a bit more than Warhol. His films, especially *Trash*, have more of a line to them.

CUKOR: They tell a story, yes. And their performances are brilliant. Joe Dallesandro does some enormously difficult things—walking around in the nude in a completely unselfconscious way, that scene when he talks to the baby in *Flesh*, and when he gives himself an overdose of heroin in *Trash*. . . . He really made me understand, more than any other film, what a drug addict was. The way you see him cutting himself off from all interest in life, going limp, it's chilling and it's beautifully done.

LAMBERT: And in *Flesh* he plays a hustler with such amiability and no guilt. It's the antithesis of *Midnight Cowboy*.

CUKOR: Nobody has any kind of guilt in these pictures. None of the attitudes are conventional, you never see a tear—that's extremely refreshing! I don't like sordid things, but these pictures I luxuriate in. They're so bold and undiluted and really new. After *Lonesome Cowboys*, I'll never be able to take a group of brothers, or of anybody, riding down a Western street again. When Beatrice Lillie "did" Ruth Draper, I could never see Ruth Draper again, she was finished for me. And *Lonesome Cowboys* finishes the Western. I love the *swank* of it all—not bothering about details, the *dégagé* act of taking a Western street, not redressing it, letting tourists walk about in the background. And I love it when the "plot" comes in. Do you remember when one of the brothers suddenly says, "My parents were killed by Apaches, of course"? That "of course" is brilliant, it's real satire.

LAMBERT: The way of bringing in "plot" satirizes plot itself.

CUKOR: Exactly. And I relish the moments of unexpected deliciousness—Viva playing a rather emotional scene to the sheriff, who's calmly making up and getting into drag. There's such a candor about these pictures, and nobody has any reserve at all. I'm just full of admiration for them.

Two-Faced Woman
(1941)

CUKOR: Usually, when you make a picture that doesn't turn out well, it's soon happily buried. Except, of course, that television keeps popping up and you may be confronted with your past failures. The funny thing about *Two-Faced Woman* is that because of Garbo it also appears at film festivals. People tell me, "It's very interesting." Well, I think it's lousy! The script was bad—not funny. We all knocked ourselves out, but it just wasn't funny. That's the whole story.

LAMBERT: Did anyone think the script was funny before you started shooting? (*Cukor looks dubious*) How did it ever get off the ground?

CUKOR: That's a long and complicated story. (*Sighs*) Let's call it "just one of those things." Even while we were doing it, it had a chill, a portent of failure. And it was most unfortunate, because Garbo was in a very brilliant period at that time.

LAMBERT: Even if the script had been better, don't you think she was a little old for the part?

CUKOR: I think you say that because the picture wasn't any

Garbo prepares
(*Two-Faced Woman*)

Ruth Gordon and
Garbo in *Two-Faced
Woman*

good. When it's not good and not funny, everything else goes, everything looks wrong. If it had been good, she'd have been radiant.

LAMBERT: Is it true that she gave up the screen because the picture failed?

CUKOR: Not really. It made her very careful about what she'd do next, and for a few years she couldn't find anything. . . . Then she decided to do a picture in Rome, *La Duchesse de Langeais*— and unfortunately that turned out to be a different kind of painful experience. It all fell apart.

LAMBERT: The money ran out?

CUKOR: Yes, and all kinds of things went wrong. It was agonizing, and she felt completely humiliated. (*Pause*) You know, I really *cringe* when people say, "I saw *Two-Faced Woman*, it was very interesting." The awful thing is, they're not being polite. They mean it.

Interlude:
On Ways of Seeing

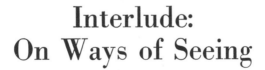

CUKOR: Anyone who looks at something special in a very original way makes you see it that way forever. The South Seas didn't exist until Somerset Maugham created that world. His vision was so accurate that I *have* to see them that way. It's like nature following art. I go to France and see a row of plane trees beside a river. I'm sure they've been there a long time, but unless the post-Impressionists had painted them, I'd never have really *seen* them. During World War Two I worked on propaganda films for the Army. William Saroyan was working there, too, and we used to have breakfast together in a café. Suddenly it was a Saroyan play, I saw the lovable, sentimental little man who ran the place, and, of course, he philosophized. I couldn't see this kind of café except through Saroyan's eyes. Before I made *Pat and Mike* I watched Bill Tilden play tennis. Eight hundred years ago I'd played the game myself, and all I remembered was balls coming at me in the most unexpected way. Now, through Tilden's eyes and motions, I could see what the whole game was about, and it seemed very simple—he was always where the ball should be. There was noth-

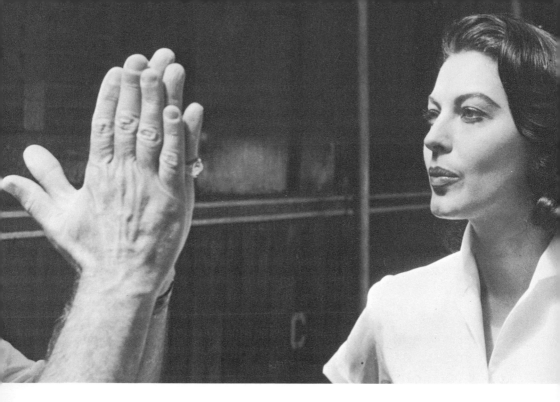

Cukor's hands, seen by Ava Gardner

ing hurried, nothing out of control. That left its imprint. I bought a painting by Grant Wood, and now all of Iowa looks like that painting to me. I'm not an addict of rock music, but when I saw the film *Woodstock* it was such a clever assemblage of everything to do with a rock festival that I came out feeling I'd seen that world. That's because the man who made the film didn't go there like a newsman, with a preconceived notion of what it was going to be like, but he looked at it like an artist and showed me something unique. I feel I know what that's all about, the way young people get a strength from each other now, the comfort and closeness of rubbing elbows. Whenever I see Wilshire Boulevard, I remember Jean Renoir saying to me, "How can you do anything about Wilshire Boulevard? There's just no smell to it." So I *know* about Wilshire Boulevard and why nothing can be done with it. And after seeing Fellini's *Satyricon*, there's only one way I can think of ancient Rome. . . . So all these things accumulate and other people's visions become a part of you.

[160]

A Woman's Face
(1941)

L AMBERT: The first half of this picture is quite fascinating, a character study of a woman whose face has been scarred since childhood and who takes her bitterness out on the world. Then the second half turns into just conventional suspense.

CUKOR: I know, rather embarrassing, but very much in the tradition of the time. What's the modern equivalent of that, by the way? A long, stirring speech on social questions, I suppose, instead of a chase—or the blind girl falling in love with the black man, and the scene when she finds out. . . . Anyway, in *A Woman's Face* the idea is how physical ugliness distorts you, like *The Happy Hypocrite*. But it's true the second part has nothing to do with the first. You see her as a monster, then plastic surgery makes her beautiful and she just wants to live down the past and become an awfully nice governess!

LAMBERT: At first, when she has something to work with, Joan Crawford is very impressive.

CUKOR: Yes, and then all the interesting character disappears. . . . (*Pause*) No, that's not *quite* fair. There's this situation when the people from her past make her try to kill the child, and maybe she will—don't you get some feeling of the struggle inside her?

LAMBERT: Not enough, I'm afraid. Everything is really blamed on the demonic influence of Conrad Veidt. It's tipped early on that she'd like to escape from her past.

CUKOR: Well, all that is not particularly well directed or well played or well written. In the first part she's really a complete character, not the actress who's playing it. Then, when she becomes pretty, she becomes . . . Joan Crawford. (*A moment of reflection*) But I would say, if I'd been making this picture now, knowing what I know, having heard your criticism, I could have managed to do it! That same girl—we'd break it in half, *show* that we intended her to become a different person, and give the struggle within her the same texture as the first half.

LAMBERT: I wonder if you could do it without considerable changes in the script. The same thing happened with the same actress in *Susan and God*. As you say, it was a convention of the period. You set up an interesting character, you start getting her into trouble, and then you see the script wheels turning in their tracks to reach a silly happy ending. And the character turns into just another movie heroine.

CUKOR: In this kind of situation you can still watch the actress for touches of the movie queen sneaking in—artificial eyelashes, lifting the breasts, all that kind of nonsense.

LAMBERT: As it is, the first hour is full of striking things. I like the way you hold back from a shot of Crawford's face until the first flashback to the restaurant. You establish something a bit raffish about that restaurant—two lesbians dancing together, and so on—and then cut to this dark stairway with a woman coming down. She steps slowly into the light, and you finally see her face, scarred and nervously defiant. Then we learn the restaurant is just a front, her real thing is heading that weird gang of thieves. They're frightened of her and at the same time make terrible snide allusions to her face. All of this reveals both sides of the woman so well, the revolting and the touching. She's tough and bitter, and then comes an awful moment when she unexpectedly catches sight of herself in a mirror. . . . One scene that Crawford plays very effectively—and I'm sure the idea was yours—is the long

A Woman's Face: Ona Munson, Joan Crawford

speech about her childhood, the drunken father and the accident that left her scarred. It's so deadpan, so lacking in self-pity.

CUKOR: I'll tell you what that was. The audience has been built up to this moment—"Now, come on, tell me the story, what's the mystery about you, why, why?" It occurred to me, what she has to say is so dramatic, she mustn't do any acting. I told her, "Just speak the lines as if you're saying the multiplication table." Then she did it, and I said, "No, no, Joan, it's still got emotion, I want no emotion at all, just say it. The audience will do the rest." And finally that's how she did it, and did it very well. Years later I saw the same kind of thing when I was going back to the theater (after twenty-seven years!) to direct *The Chalk Garden*. (There were a lot of problems and I withdrew, but I must tell you I'd just got back from a fascinating experience in India, doing *Bhowani Junction* and directing hundreds of people, and the theater seemed so *piddling*. . . .) I was working with Gladys Cooper, an actress who's had the most wonderful training in the world. And there was a situation that I watched her play with the greatest pleasure. Upstairs in the house a butler was dying. She was terribly fond of him, but the moment they told her he was dead, she reacted with a calm that was thrilling. She avoided every bit of emotion, and yet the situation was so strong it overwhelmed you. You'd *admire* a person who behaved like that. Isn't it funny what you learn from life? You see people behave wonderfully in difficult circumstances, but when you have to stage something like it on the screen, there's always the temptation to be showmanlike. You begin by using your training and thinking, "Wouldn't it be very effective this way?" And then suddenly a most extraordinary idea occurs to you. You say, "Why not do it the way it really happened?" That's what we must always hang onto.

LAMBERT: An interesting thing comes up when we discuss one of your pictures in which the material has dated. You always remind me of the conventions of the period and your principle of loyalty to the material you've decided to take on. When the conventions and the material are valid, sticking close to the times is a great strength. When they're not, you pay the penalty later.

CUKOR: That's accurate. There are certain pictures that look very impressive today, for the reasons you mention. But we might be in for a surprise seeing them ten years from now.

LAMBERT: Have you ever worried that the more immediate you are, the more you risk becoming dated?

CUKOR: No. In all the cases you bring up, people really *did* behave that way at the time, or wanted to. We may have glamorized them, we may not have represented it as well as we should, but we reflected some kind of ideal. That's the point. I recently saw a British picture about World War Two, *The Way to the Stars*. It was so pukka, I thought, "They can't be on the level!" But they were. In those days the British were making a great point of being pukka.

LAMBERT: The notion of bravery with class. Most of the British war pictures were trying to boost public morale, too.

CUKOR: Now show the white fellow! You can laugh now, but it was a human aspiration.

LAMBERT: And the great power of popular movies has been in making conventional ideas look very glamorous.

CUKOR: Yes, yes! Some old pictures I see on television, they're such a comfort. I saw Bette Davis playing twin sisters, one of them a good girl in love with a lighthouse keeper—*A Stolen Life*. I saw it twice. Did one of the twins murder the other, by the way?

LAMBERT: I've forgotten, but I think the bad one allows the good one to die in an accident and then takes her place and pretends to be the good one.

CUKOR: And will the lighthouse keeper find out? The problems are so darling and sweet. Like eating a box of candy. Nothing to do with anything that's happening now.

LAMBERT: You've just defined escapism.

CUKOR: Yes, but where people make a mistake is to think of all this as just absurd. *Lady Windermere's Fan*, like *Camille*, is about a period when a woman's good name was so important. The whole play hinges on some ridiculous letters that will incriminate and ruin people. No one gives a damn now, but at the time. . . . One has to take into account what was really going on, for better or for worse. People keep on saying now, "At least we're more honest." But what does that really mean? I don't think it's enough. Honesty can look just as silly as anything else ten years later.

Her Cardboard Lover
(1942)

LAMBERT: This is a minor film, I think you'll agree, and until the last half hour a very entertaining, straightforward adaptation of a play. The situation is typically French boulevard—a woman hires a man to impersonate her lover, he falls in love with her and refuses to leave the house—but you set it up so lightly and charmingly. Then, on the screen at any rate, the material runs thin.

CUKOR: Truth to tell, the play was in two acts, and the second act was the weaker. It was a long confrontation scene of a woman trying to get out of her own house and this man stopping her.

LAMBERT: But I liked that! The trouble is what happens afterward. I imagine the screenwriters tacked on a third act, involving a pretty, unfunny slapstick fight between the lover and the husband?

CUKOR: Yes, I remember that now with shame. Put a black mark against me for letting it happen. . . . I've told you how fascinating Laurette Taylor was in the part when I directed it on the stage. I remember she had a sort of virtuoso telephone scene, an aria on the telephone with her husband. She gives in, she lets him win her back, and it ends in absolute humiliation. Didn't Norma Shearer do that very well in the film, too?

LAMBERT: One of her best moments, and the scene is a gift to any actress with talent. (If anyone made an anthology of movie telephone scenes, by the way, it would be headed by this one and Joan Fontaine in *The Women*.) Norma Shearer was a very appealing actress, with a surprising amount of technique and a beautiful voice. Even though high comedy wasn't the easiest thing for her, she's adorable in this part.

CUKOR: And Bob Taylor gives a wonderful comedy performance.

LAMBERT: The scene of their first meeting in the casino, when he drives her up the wall by simply refusing to go away, is really a little classic of light comedy acting and direction. It's got so much invention and business and movement.

CUKOR: I garnered and stole a lot of things from the original production, you know.

LAMBERT: But it's a pity the film wasn't done in period. It's so

Shearer prepares (*Her Cardboard Lover*)

much of the twenties, like *Private Lives*. I suppose, in the forties the twenties didn't seem far enough away to be "period"?

CUKOR: In fact, the line of demarcation wasn't too clear, because the play had also been revived in London just ten years before. This kind of thing can be tricky anyway. Not long ago Leslie Caron came to my house and said, "This is a perfect forties room!" Then some very young people came and they looked around and said, "It's very rare you find a place like this intact, most of them have been destroyed. . . ." As if I was living in a museum! Maybe that's why there's always been a fear in movie studios that the audience doesn't respond to period pieces, doesn't know how to take them.

Keeper of the Flame
(1942)

CUKOR: I thought this picture opened in a most interesting way, with a lot of visual detail. And yet it wasn't very satisfactory as a whole. I don't know why. It was really very well done, but. . . . (*A gleam of thought*) I suspect the story was basically fraudulent.

LAMBERT: I agree. You conceal the fraudulence very successfully for the first hour or so.

CUKOR (*a sigh*): And then there's a fire—*and* a chase.

LAMBERT: And a noble death. But the point of departure is very intriguing. Like *Kane*, the picture opens in Gothic style with the death of a "respected national figure." A journalist who admires him tries to get his wife and private secretary to cooperate in writing his biography. They have to conceal the fact he was an undercover Fascist. All this is very credible and exciting. Then the script wants us to believe that Robert Forrest had actually built up a vast secret organization and was about to press the button and turn the country over to Fascism before he died. That's too much.

CUKOR: We made this picture during a period of undercover

Keeper of the Flame: Katharine Hepburn ("Kate's last romantic glamor girl part"), Howard da Silva, Spencer Tracy

Fascism in this country, you know. Certain things were in the air but hadn't come out into the open. I suppose, to draw attention to them we exaggerated.

LAMBERT: But the film is still full of chilling contemporary echoes. The attack on hero worship really strikes home, the idea that it turned Forrest into a Fascist. The glimpses of the dead man's effect on youth look frighteningly real—the funeral with all those sullen Boy Scouts in attendance, the secretary mouthing official phrases about a great patriot. The suggestion of a young right wing in the making is the same thing that you touched on, in a comic way, in *Susan and God*. And Katharine Hepburn as the great man's widow has definite Jacqueline Kennedy overtones.

Keeper of the Flame: directing Hepburn

CUKOR: Except that she's more mysterious and stately. It was Kate's last romantic glamor girl part.

LAMBERT: At first she seems too mannered, as if she hasn't got hold of the part, and then she warms up.

CUKOR: Well, in her first scene she had to float in wearing a long white gown and carrying a bunch of lilies. That's awfully tricky, isn't it? And doesn't she give long, piercing looks at his portrait over the mantel? (*Shrugs*) Well! . . . I think she finally carried a slightly phony part because her humanity asserted itself, and her humor. They always did. At the start her career could have gone one way or the other. After *A Bill of Divorcement* she made something called *Christopher Strong* and wore tight, glittering dresses. Then she did *Little Women*, dropping the glamor girl thing and showing the touching idealistic side of herself. It's fascinating to watch what happens to people.

LAMBERT: I can see it needed all her humanity to bring off this part. There's a waxwork quality about it.

CUKOR: About the whole film, I'm afraid. The original novel was a bit hokey-pokey and pretentious. And we shot everything on the sound stage, even the outdoor scenes.

LAMBERT: The one set that looks really fake is the exterior of the Forrest mansion with the broken bridge in the foreground.

CUKOR: I don't know why the hell we didn't get a real broken bridge and go out and shoot it.

LAMBERT: The film is directed for melodrama, very much in the manner of *Gaslight*, with a lot of very strong atmosphere and detail—

CUKOR: But still in the lush tradition.

LAMBERT: There's some excellent acting. Spencer Tracy is marvelous as the journalist, a difficult part, with everyone always saying what a great guy he is. It's hard to keep plugging all that integrity and honesty, but you believe him. And Margaret Wycherly is quite haunting as Forrest's mother.

CUKOR (*surprised*): She is? We originally shot her scene with a wonderful actress, Pauline Lord, but for some reason it didn't work.

LAMBERT: Wychlerly plays the going in and out of madness so well. She's so real that you almost forget the melodramatic trappings—the thunderstorm going on outside, and so on. I've always admired her, I still remember her in *Victory* and *White Heat*—

CUKOR: A haunted woman. You found the right word for her. Her great success was in a thriller called *The Thirteenth Chair*. She was English, she came over here and married a writer called Bayard Veiller.

LAMBERT: And their son was Anthony Veiller, who worked on several scripts for John Huston?

CUKOR: Yes. Did you notice Percy Kilbride as the taxi driver? It was his first film, before he became Pa Kettle. I like to get new people.

LAMBERT: When you're not really pleased with a film as a whole, I've noticed that you look to find something incidental to like, and very often it's the small-part actors. You're right, but all the same, as a piece of storytelling, the unfolding of a mystery, the first half of *Keeper of the Flame* is what you'd call a damn good show.

Interlude:
On Marilyn Monroe

CUKOR: There's been an awful lot of crap written about Marilyn Monroe, and there may be an exact psychiatric term for what was wrong with her, I don't know—but truth to tell, I think she was quite mad. The mother was mad, and poor Marilyn was mad. I know people who say, "Hollywood broke her heart," and all that, but I don't believe it. She was very observant and tough-minded and appealing, but she had this bad judgment about things. She adored and trusted the wrong people. She was very courageous— you know that book, *Twelve Against the Gods*? Marilyn was like that, she had to challenge the gods at every turn, and eventually she lost.

LAMBERT: When you directed her in *Let's Make Love*, did you have any inkling of the serious trouble coming?

CUKOR: I knew that she was reckless. I knew that she was willful. She was very sweet, but I had no real communication with her at all. You couldn't get at her. She was very concerned about a lot of rather pretentious things (she'd done a lot of shit-ass studying), and I'd say, "But, Marilyn, you're so accomplished, you do things that are frightfully difficult to do." She had this absolute, unerring touch with comedy. In real life she didn't seem funny, but she had this touch. She acted as if she didn't quite understand why it was funny, which is what made it so funny. She could also do low comedy—pratfalls and things like that—but I think her friends told her it wasn't worthy of her. As a director, I really had very little influence on her. All I could do was make a climate that was agreeable for her. Every day was an agony of struggle for her, just to get there. It wasn't just willfulness, it was . . . like the comedy, something she didn't seem to understand. In certain ways she was very shrewd. I once heard her talk in her ordinary voice, which was quite unattractive. So she invented this appealing baby voice. Also, you very seldom saw her with her mouth closed, because when it was closed she had a very determined chin, almost a different face. The face wasn't all that pretty, but it moved in a wonderful way, it was a wonderful movie face.

LAMBERT: I get a great sense of contradiction in what you say—how sweet she was and how tough, how shrewd and how helpless.

CUKOR: That's how it was. She could be very articulate, she knew a great deal of what it was all about, yet she took all this bad advice. And then she could be so endearing, with such beautiful manners. We were shooting one day and two young girls came on the stage, sisters of somebody I knew who'd been killed. Ordinarily Marilyn was very fussy about people coming on the stage, but this time she came up to me and said, "Please introduce me to your friends." The two girls burst into tears, and Marilyn insisted on having her picture taken with them and told them how beautiful they were. She was absolutely adorable with them. And then she could be so maddening. Before I really knew her, she was studying with Constance Collier, and the three of us were to meet at Constance's, but she was so late that I had to leave. I was leaving for Europe the next day, and I had an uncle, a very distinguished lawyer, eighty-five years old, coming to lunch. And then Marilyn called and said, "Please, I want to see you, please let me come to lunch." I expected to be stood up again, but she came—wearing her usual costume, a sweater and a mink coat—and she absolutely enchanted my old uncle. She even sent him a picture of herself. (His housekeeper told me he had a tough time

going to sleep, she'd upset him so much!) She could be a real charmer.

LAMBERT: How conscious do you think all this was?

CUKOR: I think she just behaved the way she felt at the moment; she couldn't do otherwise. Another time it was very different. Khrushchev was here, and Twentieth Century-Fox put on a lunch for him at the studio. Khrushchev's patience was tried on all occasions. It began when he arrived here and the dumb mayor of Los Angeles insulted him by saying, "You think you're going to wipe us off the face of the earth, but you're not," and then at the lunch, Spyros Skouras kept on challenging him and said, "I was just a poor boy and now I'm head of a studio." And Khrushchev said, "I was just a poor boy and now I'm head of Russia." But finally he got quite angry and said, "You won't let me go to Disneyland, I'll send the hydrogen bomb over," and frankly I wondered why he didn't. Anyway, after the lunch we went over to a sound stage where they were supposed to be shooting a picture, but they had no film in the camera, they were just going through the motions. They had bleachers for us to sit in and watch the performance. You know when a play is unsuccessful how there's a terrible hollow ring in the theater? Well. . . . The studio was trying to do its best for something called *Can Can*, and I thought it rather ill-advised to show Khrushchev and his wife what we call Frenchy stuff. Anyway, we had to climb these bleachers. Judy Garland was sort of around, and she sat with Marilyn and me. *Everything* was difficult for Judy Garland at that time—there was this big hole between each row of seats, and she was convinced she was going to fall down one of them. . . . So we watched this disaster, which ended with the girls showing us their asses—covered, of course. It became like one of those hysterical days at school when anything anybody says seems terribly funny. (Billy Wilder said, "If we show Khrushchev *Blue Denim* after this, he'll declare war.") But Marilyn, she just sat there looking dazed. It was an extraordinary occasion and you had to find it funny, but she couldn't make any connection with it.

LAMBERT: Is it true, too, that she found it very hard to concentrate when she was working?

With Marilyn Monroe

On the set (which is a replica of Cukor's own house) for *Something's Got to Give*, the Marilyn Monroe film that was never finished

CUKOR: Oh, yes. And though she was rather modest, in a curious way, she could also have that total exhibitionist thing. I remember she insisted on using one dress for a number, just one layer of chiffon with a very sketchy pair of drawers. We had to keep strong lights on her to take out the detail. The script girl said, "We've got to watch that five-o'clock shadow. . . ." She either couldn't or wouldn't control herself. She wouldn't match things— you know, when you have a cigarette in one scene, and when you cut to the close shot, you can't not have the cigarette. She simply couldn't bother with this. And she couldn't sustain scenes. She'd do three lines and then forget the rest, she'd do another line and then forget everything again. You had to shoot it piecemeal. But curiously enough, when you strung everything together, it was complete. She never could do the same thing twice, but, as with all the true movie queens, there was an excitement about her. Like Ava Gardner, she'd go from place to place and carry this excitement with her. I remember once she'd arrived late for work again, and I was annoyed, and then I watched her run across the stage in high heels (she always wore high heels), and it was so beautiful to watch, I just enjoyed watching her running and forgave her. . . . But if she was a victim of any kind, she was a victim of friends.

LAMBERT: One feels that all those people who wrote articles after her death saying Hollywood had destroyed her would have given her disastrous advice in real life.

CUKOR: Yes, yes! It may have been tough for her, but it's tough for everybody. A beautiful friend of mine killed herself years ago and Zoë Akins said, "It was the only ending for her." I think it was the only ending for Marilyn, and I think she knew it. You know where the poor darling is buried? You go into this cemetery past an automobile dealer and past a bank building, and there she lies, right between Wilshire Boulevard and Westwood Boulevard, with the traffic moving past.

Gaslight
(1944)

LAMBERT: For me, *Gaslight* is one of your best pictures and one of the best melodramas ever made. It begins with the decor, which is so imaginatively used. That nineteenth-century London house has a real menace in all its clutter and bric-a-brac.

CUKOR: Those sets are an example of the dazzling resources of a big studio. I don't think we had to go out and get any of the pieces of the period; they were all there. The research was easy. The basic question was to get a concept and then execute it with taste and savvy. At the time there was a man working here called Huldchinsky, a German refugee, a very nice and rather nervous man. His family had owned newspapers, his wife had owned railroads, and now he was working in a rather obscure position, setdressing at Metro. They'd ask him to do gas stations and stuff like that, but I knew he had this great knowledge. It required a certain amount of breaking the law. You'd say, "Well, now, this is the man I want to do it." And then comes the crucial moment when you see the set for the first time—you've insisted on a certain person doing it and it's not quite right. The establishment says, "I told you so, he can't do it." It can be quite a hassle.

LAMBERT: But this time you insisted.

CUKOR: Oh, yes. I said, "This man knows what he's doing." They were going to send in the rescue squad, you know, the old firm, and do it the old, routine way. But the stuff was *there*. You just had to take a firm stand and get the right personnel to work with you. And once you made it clear what you wanted and how desperately you wanted it, the studio would go with you.

LAMBERT: Aside from the decor, the film is beautifully acted. Was this Angela Lansbury's first appearance, either in a play or movie?

CUKOR: Yes. We'd looked for a girl for some time. John van Druten had done the script with Walter Reisch, and they were a very happy couple. In those days there were, somehow, happy collaborations. It was the day of the professionals, before everybody had to make a statement or whatever. Anyway, Van Druten said, "Moyna MacGill* is out here, she's a refugee with three children, and one of them is a girl about fourteen years old." Then we discovered that Moyna MacGill's daughter was in fact about sixteen or seventeen and had a temporary job making Christmas packages at Bullock's department store. (*A smile*) This is a Cinderella story. We sent for her and she appeared, rather nervous. She'd never acted before, but I made a test of her and thought she was awfully good. Then there was a lot of discussion because the studio didn't think she was sexy enough. (*Another smile*) I'm the hero of this story. While they were still arguing, I telephoned her and said, "Miss Lansbury, I don't know whether you're going to get the job, but you're a very talented actress." And then everyone was suddenly happy and she was cast. On the first day of shooting, even though she was only seventeen and had no experience, she was immediately professional. Suddenly I was watching real movie acting. She *became* this rather disagreeable little housemaid—even her face seemed to change, it became somehow lopsided, and mean and impertinent. I was delighted with her from the start. One day we were shooting the little scene in which she first comes to the house to apply for a job, and Charles Boyer interviews her and takes her on, and she

---

* British theater actress.

has to be introduced to the cook. We needed this scene with the cook to be written, and Van Druten was there and sat down and wrote this scene that was so good for her in three minutes flat. Angela was very sullen with the cook, who thought she was a bad lot but didn't say so. Then the cook leaves the room, and Angela says with a touch of intimacy to Boyer, "She's a real Tartar, isn't she?" And then, like an afterthought, "I won't share a room with her!" (*One of his gleaming, ironic looks*) Nothing's new, is it? Today they'd call that *improvisational*. But I wasn't the *auteur*, don't forget that. Van Druten was the *auteur*.

LAMBERT: I liked the prologue very much. The scenes set up very skillfully how your protagonists meet, and you show how blooming and confident the Ingrid Bergman character was at first.

CUKOR: It was a good scenario because it moved out of the confines of the stage.

LAMBERT: And Bergman is at her very best. It's not an easy part, because after the first few scenes she has to act being constantly frightened. Yet she never bores you with it, she finds so many variations in the fear.

CUKOR: She won the Academy Award. I like the point that she wasn't normally a timid woman; she was healthy. To reduce someone like that to a scared, jittering creature is interesting and dramatic. You have to avoid letting people play scenes before you get to them. It would have been very dangerous to cast the kind of actress you'd *expect* to go mad, the kind you know from the first moment you're in for a big mad scene....

LAMBERT: In some ways *Gaslight* is your most disguised adaptation of a play.

CUKOR: It's a movie in the best movie tradition, and I always forget when I say how many plays I've made into movies that this is one of them. That's the skill of the scenario, too; it seems to move up and down and around. There are, of course, things that make me wince a little. Whenever you see a London street, or Big Ben, it's always foggy.

LAMBERT: But a stylized fog, a movie tradition fog, in keeping with everything else. And you maintain a very elaborate texture throughout, rich and dark and rather claustrophobic.

CUKOR: It had atmosphere, I think. And all done on the back

lot. They keep on saying, "You must go to the real place," but the real place isn't always useful. It's good for certain things, obviously, but you couldn't create much of London in that period in the real place. And sometimes you can improve on the real place. After I shot the White Cliffs of Dover somewhere beyond Malibu and then saw the reality again, the real White Cliffs, they were quite disappointing.

LAMBERT: It strikes me that a new element appears in your movies starting after *The Philadelphia Story* in 1940 and culminating in this one. I know they're all melodramas, but *A Woman's Face* and *Keeper of the Flame* and *Gaslight* share this rich, virtuoso camera style. Photographically they're more adventurous, they take us into quite a different world. Could some of this be due to what was happening in Hollywood at that time—the influence of *Citizen Kane*?

CUKOR: I'm not aware of it, though I know all that was very

Victoriana: Huldchinsky's set for *Gaslight*, with Ingrid
Bergman and Charles Boyer

Gaslight: Cukor directs Angela Lansbury in her film debut

Ingrid Bergman in *Gaslight*

much in the air. I must say that I thought *Citizen Kane*, in spite of its brilliance, was rather too much UFA.* But *The Magnificent Ambersons* was superb. Of course, sometimes we know we're being influenced, and sometimes it's just the air you breathe. Maybe the kind of thing you mention was fashionable at the time, and maybe it gave people courage to be more adventurous. The same thing's happened recently with fashionable cutting, sudden transitions and no dissolves. But I really think the style comes out of the story. If you're going to do a story about a murder in a Victorian house, you make it claustrophobic, you make it clouded and gaslit. You research the period, not just to reproduce things physically, but for the emotions it stirs up in you. The earlier films you mention were all comedies. I always say the text dictates the whole style to me, which may not be to the director's advantage, because it means his touch is not immediately recognizable.

LAMBERT: You've also mentioned your distaste for violence. In these three melodramas there's practically no violence at all. Even the fight between Boyer and Joseph Cotten at the end of *Gaslight* takes place offscreen.

CUKOR: That was probably the scenario, although I've never believed in fights. I think violence is a cop-out. It's so easy to create that kind of dramatic situation—you and I are sitting here and we cut to a bomb ticking in the next room. And those wretched animal pictures which people think are so sweet! Lassie goes wandering around and suddenly there's an awful encounter with a boa constrictor or whatever. I loathe that, even more than I loathe human violence. You have to get violence and tension from the situation, rather than imposing or indulging it. And then the *chases!* I was suddenly stuck with a chase scene in *A Woman's Face*—they had to rush after each other from place to place in the snow. It seemed completely ludicrous to me. (And I let a second unit shoot quite a bit of it.) All this kind of thing is an artificial shot in the arm, and I'm surprised that some of it still persists today.

---

* It was heavily influenced by the German expressionist cinema. UFA, the major German company of the twenties and thirties, produced such films as *Metropolis, The Last Laugh, The Love of Jeanne Ney* and *The Testament of Dr. Mabuse.*

LAMBERT: At Metro, in the thirties and forties, you worked chiefly with the studio's two most famous cameramen, William Daniels (on *Dinner at Eight, Romeo and Juliet, Keeper of the Flame*) and Joseph Ruttenberg (on *The Women, The Philadelphia Story, Gaslight*). Was this by preference?

CUKOR: Not really. I worked with several others, too. Karl Freund finished *Camille* when Daniels got sick. I worked with Robert Planck on *A Woman's Face* and George Folsey on *Pat and Mike* and Freddie Young, who later did *Lawrence of Arabia*, on *Bhowani Junction*—and some others, too. In general, I found a great number of very gifted and accomplished men, but one has to give most of them the courage to take chances. You tell a cameraman, "Now, I don't want this to be one two three. Let's be bold. If it goes wrong, I'll take the blame." That gives them confidence and worked very well, as I've told you, on *A Double Life* and *A Star Is Born*. But sometimes, of course, the front office descends on you. On *David Copperfield* I had a wonderful cameraman called Oliver Marsh. He did the first few scenes in a very brilliant, rather sketchy way, exactly what I wanted. Then the front office complained the audience wouldn't be able to see it properly. Ollie said, "Oh, thank you very much," and from then on played it safe. In the earlier days, too, cameramen had to photograph the movie queens and make them look damn good. Louis B. Mayer was a great believer in his movie queens "looking right."

LAMBERT: A basic rule?

CUKOR: A basic rule! And there's no doubt it created some indestructible images.

LAMBERT: Remembering your costume pictures at that time, something occurs to me. Different cameramen photographed *David Copperfield* and *Camille* and *Gaslight*, but what one sees in all three is *your* style rather than a particular cameraman's style.

CUKOR: Really? I think there's much more of a mark in my later pictures, in color. From *A Star Is Born* onward I began working with Hoyningen-Huene and Gene Allen—

LAMBERT: Neither of whom, incidentally, were cameramen but a color adviser and an art director. I agree there's a more distinct, purely visual mark in the later pictures. But in the three costume pictures I mentioned, to say nothing of *Little Women* and *Zaza*—with different cameramen again—I see first of all your own response to the past, your own way of looking at it.

CUKOR: Now that you say it like that, I feel it's the case. And yet my work really begins and ends through the actors. And it seems to me, the more successfully you work through the actors, the more your own work disappears.

Interlude:
On the Director as Romantic

CUKOR: Years ago I went to the theater with Laurette Taylor, and there was a scene in the play when a man and a woman were rolling on the floor and biting each other and all the rest of it, and Laurette said, "They're making love the way sexually frigid people make love." You see a good deal of that in movies today, and sometimes I wonder if all the "new freedom" came about through lack of passion. (It's like the question, "Did you have sex last night?" which strikes me as obscenely chilling. You might as well ask if one took a purgative.) I've worked with a great many of the movie queens, and one thing they knew: They didn't have to prove anything by stripping or writhing on the floor. The fact that they *didn't* do this made them even more attractive. Recently, one or two of them have yielded to fashion and done exactly this, and it only diminished their allure. It was the same with the male stars, who didn't have to parade the whole thing to turn an audience on. Recently I saw again on TV *It Happened One Night*. There's a scene in which Claudette Colbert takes off her dress and is wearing what I think they used to call a combination slip. All you see is a satin strap glinting in the moonlight, and everything else is done by Clark Gable wearing pajamas. I found this created a real erotic tension. Does that mean that in the last resort I'm a romantic director?

LAMBERT: I think so. And why not?

CUKOR: Yes, why not? Romanticism in a love story doesn't have to mean harps and crinolines.

LAMBERT: Just emotion. And the great advantage of emotion, as Oscar Wilde said, is that it leads us astray.

CUKOR: And don't emotion and passion become *more* emotional and *more* passionate if you suggest them, if you indicate them, rather than just let everyone go freewheeling? I think there's a marvelous way to be a romantic, which is to catch love without people undressing.

A Double Life (1947)
Adam's Rib (1949)
Born Yesterday (1950)
The Marrying Kind (1951)
Pat and Mike (1952)
The Actress (1953)
It Should Happen to You (1954)

LAMBERT: You've collaborated with Garson Kanin and Ruth Gordon, separately or together, on seven films. For the record, Ruth and Garson are credited as having cowritten *A Double Life, Adam's Rib, The Marrying Kind* and *Pat and Mike*. Ruth adapted her own play, *The Actress*, and Garson wrote *It Should Happen to You*. I think he also did most of the work on the adaptation of his play *Born Yesterday*, though for some reason he didn't take a credit. I suppose you knew them both pretty well before you started working together?

CUKOR: I'd known of Ruth as an actress, naturally, for a long time. And we were already fast friends before she married Garson. It didn't take at first, though. Years ago, in the twenties, when I was running that stock company in Rochester, she came up to try out a play, and we didn't get on at all well. She says that when she saw the movie of *The Philadelphia Story* she was so delighted that she sent me a wire, and that's when our friendship really began. I think I first met Garson Kanin at some Screen Directors' Guild function, and he was so bright and so nice that I asked him to lunch. It was a small party, and he sat between Vivien Leigh and Laurence Olivier, and they went home together and I don't think they left each other for years. The first of the films we did together was *A Double Life*, for his own company. It was a very happy and very equal collaboration, Ruth and Garson worked very closely together—no question of a writer trying to get his wife a job. Garson was a brilliant playwright and screen-writer and had the enormous advantage of knowing his *métier* very well—he'd already directed some successful comedies. Many of the lovely directorial touches in our films together were in the script. (I know this won't sit well with those people who believe in the *auteur* theory, but these films just didn't have one *auteur*.) Ruth and Garson lived in New York then, but they would come out here for long stretches of time and write, and we'd have readings here and they'd stay for the rehearsals. An interesting thing, in these days of improvisation, was how we did the ad libs. I wanted them to *sound* improvised, but I didn't believe in actu-ally improvising them. Sometimes when I was shooting a scene with several characters, a party scene or something, and we needed a few ad libs, the actors would try them and I felt they didn't work. So I called the Kanins on the phone and told them the problem, and they'd say, "All right," and call me back a little later and I'd write them down. Sometimes these ad libs were just general, but sometimes I felt they had to be more specific. For the dinner party scene in *Adam's Rib*, when a lawyer and his wife are entertaining other judges and legal people with their wives, you couldn't have them just saying, "Oh, good evening!" For things like this I'd call Ruth and Garson and tell them where the scene was going. Later, I was very pleased when people said about that scene how much they liked the small talk. I'm a great believer in that.

LAMBERT: How were these films set up with the studios? Did it begin with the Kanins writing a story, or the outline of a story, and submitting it?

CUKOR: Yes, once we knew that all three of us wanted to go ahead with something, and the studio agreed, then they'd come out here to write the screenplay. It was all very harmonious. They respected me as a director. I respected them as writers. You read all these articles and statements today demanding "complete involvement" and "personal expression" and all that, but you couldn't have been more involved than *we* were, for Chrissake! It was taken for granted, in fact. It was considered part of what you were supposed to do, and you did it happily, because you wanted to. I find this kind of language now completely egomaniacal. Instead of really creating, they're giving themselves a quick self-analysis and, rather immodestly, I find, furthering themselves and drawing attention to their own achievements. Nobody could have worked harder than the Kanins, nobody could have been more

On the set of *A Double Life*: Cukor, Ruth Gordon, Garson Kanin, Ronald Colman

involved than I was, but we didn't talk about it. But still you go on hearing and reading that we were all a lot of corrupt people going to a lot of Hollywood parties. Well, people may be happy to learn that we did a lot of agonizing, too—plenty of agonizing, I may say, at the time. But we also did it with a humor that seems to be lacking now. And while we had just as much fanaticism then, you know, as people do now, I don't think we were quite so aggressive or self-righteous about it. How else can you work, anyway, except with complete involvement? Just so long as you don't think you're going to change the world. . . . With the Kanins and myself, there was a great deal of companionship and humanity and hard work. Garson says we had rows, too, but that's all part of a complete collaboration. In the pictures with Spencer and Kate they contributed things as well—but nobody made announcements in the press.

On location for *Adam's Rib*: Cukor rehearses Judy Holliday in the New York subway

Othello offstage: Shelley Winters and Ronald Colman in *A Double Life*

LAMBERT: Your films with the Kanins were all small scale and intimate in tone. Were they low budget, too?

CUKOR: Not really. They were intimate, indeed, but what startled me when I saw *Adam's Rib* again was the variety of backgrounds—the apartment, the courtroom, the offices, the tax consultant's office, the farm, all those different New York streets. It moved around.

LAMBERT: All of them did, and in a modest way they were truly innovational. In *Adam's Rib* the opening scenes with a distracted Judy Holliday trailing her husband across New York—through the streets, in the subway—to his rendezvous with another woman are beautifully shot and vivid in what would now be called *cinéma vérité* style.

CUKOR: Throughout a great many pictures I've done we tried certain things but didn't publicize them. When Kate did a picture in Europe recently they said to her, as if it was a great innovation, "We're going to *rehearse* before shooting." And Kate said, "I came out to Hollywood forty years ago, and we rehearsed *A Bill of Divorcement* with Mr. Cukor for two weeks." In *The Marrying Kind* and *It Should Happen to You* we shot some long and tricky sequences in Central Park. In *The Marrying Kind* I must say we did a great many things—we shot dream sequences right in Times Square, scenes inside the New York post office very cleverly blended with studio work here, and a complicated scene in front of the Pennsylvania Station. And it was done as a matter of course. I'm wondering now why we never made a fanfare about it.

LAMBERT: Also, in *Adam's Rib* and *Pat and Mike* and *The Actress* there are a number of exceptionally long takes. Some of them are quite daring because they contain a lot of business and camera movement and others because they last more than five minutes and hardly anyone moves.

CUKOR: Some ran longer than that. The scene at the jail in *Adam's Rib*, where Kate interviews Judy Holliday after she's tried to kill her husband, ran nine and some minutes. There was no reason to move during it, of course—and we couldn't move anyway, it all took place in the cell. It was Judy Holliday's first scene in the picture, and in those days there was a lot of chatter about "scene stealing," but I never knew what the hell that meant. You can't steal a scene in a movie because it's all controlled by the camera and the editing. The most you can do is use some little tricks and maybe distort it. They used to say, "Judy Holliday steals scenes," but this was basically her scene. It was shot full on her, with a three-quarter view of Kate's back. Kate wasn't being generous or anything, and Judy Holliday wasn't stealing anything—it was how the text indicated the scene should be played. (And an audience knows Kate, knows her voice. You don't have to keep cutting to her.) Not only did Kate play back to camera, but she indicated, as good actresses can do, "that's the way it's supposed to be." She and Spencer always played together that way, too. It's an important element of real collaboration.

LAMBERT: Once the studio approved one of these projects, were you given almost complete independence?

CUKOR: Yes, and help, too. There were a few disagreements, a few cuts made against my wishes, but by and large a great deal of support and sympathetic understanding. We were allowed to use new people like Judy Holliday and Aldo Ray, to shoot on location wherever we wanted, and to research as long as we wanted. For instance, for *The Actress*, which is an autobiographical play about Ruth as a young girl, we went to the house in which she was brought up. There were some long scenes played in the kitchen, if you remember, a tiny kitchen with, for some reason, eight doors. They led off to this and to that, completely illogical, but we reproduced it so skillfully, so carefully, at the studio that you couldn't tell you weren't in the real place. (We didn't use the real location because we couldn't have moved the camera around in it.) And we worked out a very realistic lighting plan so that it never looked as if it was shot on a stage. And nobody objected to any of this.

LAMBERT: *A Double Life* is a backstage story in which the backstage and theater scenes are brilliant, but the story doesn't seem to me to work.

CUKOR: I wanted the photography to give the impression of what it's *like* to be on a stage giving a performance. When someone steps onto a stage for the first time, his reaction is that the light's blinding him. I thought it important for this story to transfer the audience to the stage, which meant you had to halate certain lights into the camera to give the illusion I'm talking about. Many cameramen are frightened of things like that, and you have to take the responsibility yourself if it doesn't work. I said to Milton Krasner, who did a brilliant job, "Don't worry about whatever curious effects happen, just let's try it. Let all kinds of things hit the lens as if they're hitting the audience." I think these scenes had a good deal of excitement as a result, and it helped the unreality and terror of what was going on. We also shot a lot of location scenes in New York, and they helped the atmosphere, too.

LAMBERT: All this side of the picture is so good, it's a pity the central situation doesn't convince. The idea *sounds* intriguing—a famous actor playing Othello finds the part taking over his personality, he becomes paranoiac and eventually commits murder—and maybe it looked better on paper than in reality. And Ronald Colman, excellent though he is when he's not playing Othello on the stage, lacks the kind of dark and sinister quality you needed.

CUKOR: Colman had so much equipment for a screen actor, he

Yippie-ism in court. In *Adam's Rib*, Hepburn (assisted by Hope Emerson) demonstrates the equal strength of women to Tracy. In court: David Wayne, Judy Holliday

In *Adam's Rib*, Hepburn wears the hat that Tracy ad-libs "makes you look like Grandma Moses"

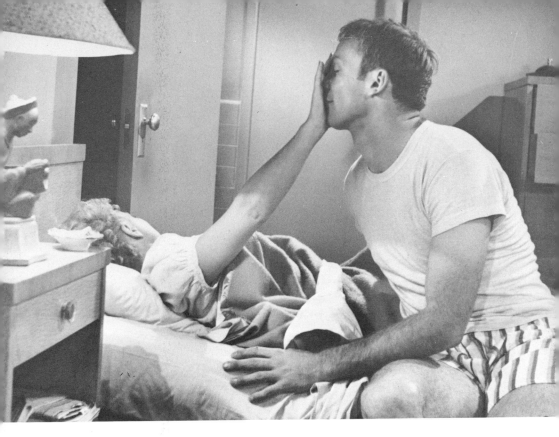

Judy Holliday and Aldo Ray in *The Marrying Kind*

was photogenic, he could move, he could give the impression of movement and yet remain perfectly still, he had this plastic quality, he'd studied Chaplin and Fairbanks. For the death scene, I was shooting from a high angle, and I told him, "When you die, all your life, everything that's happened, should come into your eyes for a brief moment." Well, he did it—or told me he did it—but I couldn't see it when we shot it. Next day, in the rushes, it was all there. He knew how to let the quality of *thought* come out. But, yes, I question whether he had the danger and the madness for a great Othello, on the stage or in real life. Some can be scary, some can't, and Colman was a most gifted actor who didn't have a sense of the demonic. But Shelley Winters, as the waitress he murders, was awfully good and awfully funny. It was her first important movie part.

LAMBERT: She made the sexiness curiously disgusting.

CUKOR: And funny, too. Do you remember the scene when Colman goes to her apartment? She makes all kinds of passes at him, which he ignores. Then she sits on the arm of his chair, and he does something very original and erotic. He runs his hand over her arm—and you know it's not a question of whether he's going to lay her or not, but that *he*'ll decide *when* he wants to. It had a "cool" that was rather ahead of its time.

LAMBERT: I also like the contrast in the settings between the world of the theater and the squalor of the places Colman goes to when the underside of his nature asserts itself. And you know the theater very well, which really shows.

CUKOR: We all knew it, Ruth and Garson and myself, but it was still mysterious to us after all this time, and I think we got that across.

LAMBERT: From one point of view *Adam's Rib* is a conventional situation comedy. A husband and wife, both lawyers, find themselves prosecuting and defending the same client. And while the personal story, how it affects their marriage and so on, is done with much liveliness within the convention, the other side, the arguments between Hepburn and Tracy about law and order, is wonderfully topical now.

CUKOR (*surprised*): Really?

LAMBERT: When I saw the picture again, Hepburn's antics in the courtroom absolutely prefigured the Chicago Seven. She introduces sideshows and absurd characters and turns the courtroom into a circus. Then Tracy argues that we've got to respect the law, we may be against it but we've got to respect it, and it's exactly like Abbie Hoffman versus Judge Hoffman.

CUKOR: That's very interesting, but I don't think Garson wrote it in a prophetic way.

LAMBERT: I'm sure not. It just shows the sharpness of the observation in the picture.

CUKOR: All their pictures were like that.

LAMBERT: It's why the courtroom scenes are so authentic. Funny and lively, and with a real freshness in the way they deal with the people and procedures involved.

CUKOR: Even though we were making a comedy, I wanted to research it. There was a murder trial going on just before we started shooting. A woman stabbed somebody. I went to the trial very often, and we took pictures of the woman from the time she was first brought in. She looked very tough and made-up before the case started, then she appeared in court very discreetly dressed and quiet and modest. (We used this idea for the Judy Holliday character.) Also, I watched what in fact did happen in a courtroom, the behavior of the judge and the jury. I got to understand the function of a judge—he's there to listen and to interpret the law and to see that the real decision is made by the jury. In so many films courtroom scenes get frozen on an almost formal level. You have to go and discover what it's really like. I did this kind of thing on all the films with Ruth and Garson. I would even go to people's apartments to pick up all those illogical details you can use in set-dressing. All our sets were reproductions of what I'd seen, which is why the films have an almost documentary feeling.

LAMBERT: There's even something documentary about the way Hepburn and Tracy play together. Because they were so close in real life, their intimacy on the screen has an extra dimension.

CUKOR: It was human. Comedy isn't really any good, isn't really funny, without that. First you've got to be funny and then, to elevate the comedy, you've got to be human. That's why anything that works as comedy should also work as tragedy, and vice versa.

LAMBERT: *The Marrying Kind* is one of those movies in which the originality creeps up on you. It starts off as light romantic comedy about two ordinary people falling in love and getting married and having a child and so on. Then, suddenly, after you reveal the death of the child, the whole tone changes. Life turns sour and everything takes on a desperate quality. The death of the child, by the way, is a brilliant sequence. Judy Holliday and Aldo Ray are having a picnic by a lake. She picks up a banjo and starts to sing a song, and the camera stays on her. You know that the little boy has gone off with some other children to swim. But the camera doesn't follow him, it stays on Judy Holliday singing this absurd song. Then, in the background, seen only from the waist down, you show the legs of people running back and forth with increasing agitation. The parents are completely unaware of it. Judy Holliday goes almost all the way through the song before you cut to her little daughter running up in panic, crying, "Joey's drowned!" It's electrifying.

CUKOR: What is also electrifying is the way Aldo Ray runs into the water for his son. I discovered he'd once been a frogman, and there's something about the way he moves in the water—not just a frantic father—there's a kind of violence to it.

LAMBERT: And the scene ends with a very effective dissolve. You come out of the flashback and return to the present, where Judy Holliday is relating this episode in the judge's room. As you dissolve, she's crying and screaming by the lake, and back in the judge's room she's reliving the moment, crying and beating her fists on the table.

CUKOR: I cribbed that from a production of *The Cherry Orchard* I'd seen years ago. If you remember, Madame What's-Her-Name comes back to her estate with her daughter, and she's very happy and gay. Then Nazimova (I've seen the play done several ways, but never this way) did something remarkable. A tall young man wearing a blouse comes into the room. Nazimova looked at him, ran over and threw herself on him, sobbing. He was the tutor of her son who'd drowned years before. Usually actresses play this moment rather sentimentally, but Nazimova gave you the impression the boy had only just been drowned. She had this beautiful, rather fragile voice, and she sobbed as if he was actually carrying the body of the child. It had a terrible stab of immediacy and I remembered it, I stored it up. I'm glad it worked. I'd even forgotten about it until now.

LAMBERT: Another thing that sets *The Marrying Kind* apart from most of your films is the very unspectacular milieu.

CUKOR: The text showed me how important that was.

LAMBERT: And you handle the ordinary, the everyday, with such authority.

CUKOR (*amused by a note of surprise he detects in this*): I was born with the powers. You must realize that. Let me tell you about the post office. Since Aldo Ray works there in the film, we shot several scenes there and made a very clever blending of the real thing and a set. If I ever had to do hell in a film—no, not quite hell, let's say purgatory—the New York post office would be the perfect setting. Such a curious life, devoid of ambition, anger, jealousy, adventure, suspense—you just sort letters and put them in sacks. In my world you run the gamut of emotions daily, so the post office seemed just nowhere. Years ago I was flying from Europe to New York and the plane stopped at Gander. When I

The Marrying Kind: Aldo Ray works in the post office ("Purgatory")

The Marrying Kind: Aldo Ray's nightmare sequence in the post office

stepped out, I found the light inside the plane and outside it was exactly the same. It was completely dead, not daylight or night. You couldn't tell where you were. I remembered this when we shot the post office. Of course, the scenes themselves were very shrewdly written.

LAMBERT: And very well played by Aldo Ray.

CUKOR: He'd never acted before, except in a test that I saw in which he played a taxi driver. He was sitting on the floor and playing a card game, and there was something about the look in his eyes, the way the light hit the skin and went into the eyes. Just for a moment he had to get angry in the scene, and I knew he was made for movies. He's Venetian Italian, blond and all that, but he looks and sounds very American. For one scene in our picture he put on a dark shirt and hat and suddenly looked Italian. He's a very gifted actor, did all the difficult things so well, cried so well—that's very difficult for a young actor—and was funny and endearing.

LAMBERT: Not afraid, either, to be unsympathetic at moments.

CUKOR: Bitter and bad-tempered, yes. And absolutely fearless as an actor. We shot a dream sequence at Broadway and Forty-second Street and I said, "You just run across Broadway in your shorts." He did it. There was nothing he wouldn't do. Incidentally, the idea of putting dream sequences into a very realistic comedy was interesting.

LAMBERT: The movie has many original aspects, and not the least of them is the ending. On the surface it looks conventionally happy. The couple has reconciled, they decide not to go through with the divorce after talking everything over with the judge, and you see them walk out into the street together. But you can't help feeling they're going back to a kind of hell.

CUKOR (*emphatically*): Yes, yes! If you believe the picture up to then, it's the only way it can hit you. I'm glad you see it that way.

LAMBERT: The second of the Hepburn-Tracy films, *Pat and Mike*, is a profoundly unassuming thing that's really a comic masterpiece.

CUKOR: *You* said that, not me, so when this book comes out—

LAMBERT: I'll stick by it.

CUKOR (*amused*): Just don't make it appear *I* said it.

The Marrying Kind: dream sequence in Times Square (Judy Holliday)

LAMBERT: What I like so much is that in dealing with a raffish, rundown side of the world of sports, and the shady character played by Tracy, the treatment is so elegant and light. Everyone in the movie except Hepburn is a bit seedy, but you portray them as if they're somehow delightful, successful people.

CUKOR: The only gangsters I could ever do are funny gangsters. I turned down a serious gangster picture once and I told them, "When gangsters come in and scare people, they never scare me." And Garson had this witty idea of a ladylike, rather high-minded female athlete who's taken on by a gangsterish manager. Kate played this so beautifully. When she first meets Spencer and his friend, she imagines they're much more serious gangsters than they really are and becomes rather like Mrs. Roosevelt, very much on her dignity and quite humorless. Then quite suddenly she does karate on them.

LAMBERT: The gangsters are very nicely written, with a nod to Damon Runyon.

CUKOR: You remember when Spencer says about Kate, "There ain't much meat on her, but what there is, is choice"? He does this with his back three-quarters to the camera and gets a big laugh just on the strength of his personality.

LAMBERT: Like *The Marrying Kind*, the movie has a documentary quality—the very exact backgrounds and the use of famous athletes playing themselves—as well as some wildly unexpected fantasy sequences. There's a brilliant scene when Hepburn's tennis game goes off because her fiancé is watching and he makes her nervous. The net is suddenly terribly high, her own tennis racket becomes the size of a tablespoon and her opponent's big as a spade.

CUKOR: You know where we got that from? Bill Tilden, one of the great tennis players, told us one day, "That's the impression you get when you're not playing well."

LAMBERT: So the fantasy is really documentary as well.

CUKOR: Yes, it was apropos, it really made a point, and I think that was quite a new idea.

LAMBERT: With, as usual, no great fuss made about it.

CUKOR: The whole thing has a *dégagé* air. It's not played from point to point, but let the chips fall where they may. When it gets a laugh it's not playing for laughs.

LAMBERT: It contains some of the most relaxed humor I've ever seen in a movie, and the most charming aspect of all is that you're basically telling a love story. The idea of these two people falling in love is improbable and yet totally right, and of course with Hepburn and Tracy playing it, you get something extra again.

CUKOR: It's an unusually discreet kind of love story.

LAMBERT: They hardly even touch each other.

CUKOR: They never do, do they?

LAMBERT: Only once. It's a purely professional physical contact when Hepburn has strained a muscle and Tracy massages her leg. There's the suggestion of a naughty-boy look on Tracy's face—he's been telling her beforehand that athletes must give up sex while in training. And Hepburn is uptight but determined not to show it.

Tracy and his two prize athletes (Aldo Ray and Katharine Hepburn) in *Pat and Mike*

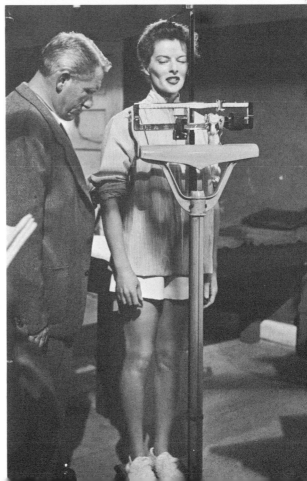

Pat and Mike: Hepburn weighs in. Tracy: "there ain't much meat on her, but where there is, is choice"

CUKOR: Chemically they're so funny together because they should have no rapport at all.

LAMBERT: And the situation wouldn't let them admit it, anyway. It's very subtly done, no nodding to the audience and saying, "Get this?"

CUKOR: And they never bring in a dirty word for laughs, as comedy usually does today. You say "shit" or whatever and people are supposed automatically to laugh. Or there's a touch of self-righteousness and the whole thing is really about helping the blacks. . . . Maybe the way life is now, comedy is bound to be heavily written and heavily played. (*A pause*) I remember the readings we had here, in this room, for this picture. Spence sat in a corner, his glasses on, and read absolutely brilliantly. Kate read her part, and Ruth and Garson and I took the others. It was a most happy period for everybody.

LAMBERT: It's a very sharp idea behind *It Should Happen to You*, the publicity hunger on the part of people who've got no real qualifications, people who just want to be somebody famous. And Judy Holliday plays it marvelously. She's so basically dumb, yet she has this horrifying shrewdness and determination about getting somewhere. When she's saved up enough money to rent a huge billboard at Columbus Circle with her name on it and she just drives around and around it, infatuated with it, the scene is very funny but also chilling.

CUKOR: The idea of becoming a great celebrity without being able to do *anything* is a very important notion. Publicity can really do it, too. Today it makes Presidents. It's really the name of the game. The other night I was watching television, and I saw a darling girl, Jane Fonda, who's going on about the Indians and everything right now. She was a guest on Mr. Cavett's show, and he's very bright and witty, and together they were solving the Indian question. Then on came a very distinguished old gentleman who turned out to be the Archbishop of Canterbury. I thought, "Christ Almighty, what's *he* doing here?" Mr. Cavett was polite to him, but with no cathedral hush in the voice at all. The archbishop started talking, and he made some reference to "all Christendom" and then, as a kind of afterthought, to "all the other religions." Jane got rather feisty about him putting down the other religions in this way, and he tried to explain, but she just wasn't having it, and she answered, "That's what *you* say." And I thought, why would the archbishop appear on this thing? And why would Jane argue with him? And what is the point? Well, *It Should Happen to You* is a kind of exposé of this.

LAMBERT: In fact, there's a scene after Judy Holliday has become famous—for having done nothing except put her name on this billboard—when she's invited to appear on a TV show with other female celebrities. There's Constance Bennett and Ilka Chase—

CUKOR (*amused*): And a former actress called Wendy Barrie. Remember *her*?

LAMBERT: Yes. And you made this picture fifteen years ago, so the look of a TV show is different, but nothing has really changed. The women talk a lot but say nothing.

CUKOR: Nothing at all. They pretend to be very original, but they're just rather tricky about putting themselves across. All that crappy, fatuous "personality" and laughing and first-name basis!

LAMBERT: Everything's false, including the atmosphere of friendship.

CUKOR: And the wit—completely hokey-pokey! The clothes were very good in that sequence, too, Judy Holliday wearing that off-the-shoulder chiffon gown and picture hat, like a romantic celebrity.

LAMBERT: Another documentary touch.

CUKOR: All these films by Garson and Ruth are about something. . . . We shot a lot in New York, we used Central Park as a character, as we did in *The Marrying Kind,* and this time it was during a heat wave, which brings all the mad people out. You can see lots of mad people in the park and sitting on steps in front of houses. And it was Jack Lemmon's first chance; he'd been a television actor before. When we came to shoot the scene when he and Judy Holliday have a row in a restaurant, they rehearsed it and did it very well, but I said, "I don't believe it, I don't believe one damn thing. Jack, what do you do when you get angry?" He said, "I get chills and cramps, I get sick to my stomach, but you can't use that." "Oh," I said, "do that!" So in the height of fury he suddenly clutches his stomach, and it makes all the difference.

LAMBERT: That's one of your trademarks, making a scene look spontaneously improvised.

CUKOR: You have to watch for all the little things and catch them when they're real. There's also the scene when Peter Lawford is trying to seduce Judy Holliday, chasing her around the room. He gets her on the couch, starts nuzzling her neck—very erotically, as if he were taking her clothes off. Then he takes one of her earrings off and puts it on the table so he can nuzzle her ear. Very erotic, too—she's terrified but rather excited. She picks up the earring and tries to escape. He chases her again, and she ends up on the couch, in the same position, with the earring back on. It so happened we had a property man on the picture who'd worked with The Three Stooges. He said, "I have an idea, may I help on this?" I said, "Please do," and he suggested, "Let *her* take the earring off herself, so he can nuzzle her ear." So we did, and it made a terribly funny moment. Later in the scene she had to pour champagne down Peter Lawford's neck. We only had four shirts for Peter Lawford, so we could only shoot four takes, and it was tricky for the camera. On the last take I said, "Judy if you laugh, I'll just kill you, I'll kill you dead." Well, she didn't laugh, but she giggled, and it was absolutely great. I asked if she'd done it deliberately, in spite of what I'd said, and she didn't really know. Sometimes you get these very human things on the set.

LAMBERT: There's an episode toward the end of *It Should Happen to You* which rather spoils the last twenty minutes for me. I attribute it to Garson, because there's an echo of the same thing, completely out of left field, in *The Marrying Kind*. It's about *why* Judy Holliday gives up her publicity drive and settles for a more realistic life. Lemmon says to her, "Why do you want all this, anyway? Don't be above the crowd, be a part of the crowd." There's an implication here of keeping the "little people" in their place. In *The Marrying Kind*, Aldo Ray asks his brother-in-law for advice: Should he allow his wife to accept a legacy that her ex-boss left her in his will? The brother-in-law goes into a monologue of which the gist is, "Your trouble is that you're too ambitious. I'm a butcher and happy being a butcher, and I don't want anything more."

CUKOR: I don't think Garson believes that at all. He's all for success.

LAMBERT: I thought so. And why not? It's just that both moments have nothing to do with the story and sound message-y.

CUKOR: The wrong message.

LAMBERT: In *It Should Happen to You* it would have been

Jean Simmons as the young Ruth Gordon in *The Actress*

Judy Holliday and Jack Lemmon in *It Should Happen to You*

much more convincing if Judy Holliday gives up because she realizes the publicity hunger is driving her nuts and wrecking her life.

CUKOR: You're right. The other way shows no tolerance for starters.

CUKOR: In *The Actress*, I remember, the same kind of personal moment occurred that I told you about in *It Should Happen to You*. Jean Simmons is in her bedroom, chattering away with her little girlfriend about the theater. Spencer Tracy, who plays her father, comes in unexpectedly. He finds out she's spent fifty cents on a theater magazine and he's furious with her. Talk about people who can be scary, Spence could be scary. He and Jean Simmons adored each other, but when we rehearsed the scene his anger was so real that she started giggling. "I know I'm old and I'm not much good," Spence said, "but does this broad have to laugh in my face?" "No, keep it in, Jean," I said. "When you're absolutely terrified you piss yourself with a kind of laughter. It's real."

LAMBERT: *The Actress* has a lot of that very intimate, very spontaneous feeling, but in other ways it's different from your other pictures with the Kanins. It's a period piece, a piece of Americana, and its qualities are nostalgia and charm. I like it very much and I like Jean Simmons very much, even though I think she's miscast. As the young Ruth Gordon with a desperate desire to go on the stage she lacks the fierceness and the very personal energy and the offbeat look.

CUKOR: Yes, if a girl like Jean Simmons says, "I want to go on the stage," it's no great surprise. Obviously she's lovely, and she probably should. I'm sure with Ruth it was much more difficult. Of course, this was the Hollywood tradition at the time. Nobody was ever *really* plain—either plain girls were played by Olivia de Havilland or they wore glasses, and then someone took the glasses off and they were ravishing beauties. I suppose there were no actresses, or no name-actresses, anyway, around at the time who were absolutely right. In a sense it's conventional casting. About the fierceness—the producer made some minor cuts, they were only details, but they did soften Ruth's character, they played down her terrific determination-at-all-costs. I remember Ruth very much objecting to these changes, and she was right.

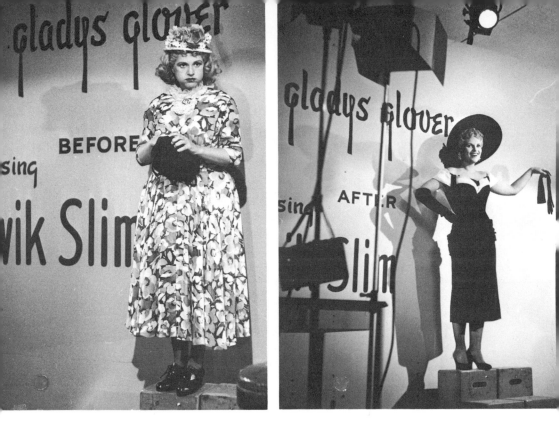

At the height of her fame, Gladys Glover does a before-and-after
commercial. Judy Holliday in *It Should Happen to You*

LAMBERT: The film bears some other signs of cutting, too. Not
just details, but in the narrative—

CUKOR: There was a very pernicious habit—when you finished
a picture, *everybody* had a panacea! People who hadn't contributed very much would say, "Oh, you can cut this and that,
and you'll fix everything." I think the studio was a bit worried
about the box-office career of *The Actress*, so they started fixing.

LAMBERT: How did the picture do commercially?

CUKOR: Not particularly well. But none of the cuts were helpful, commercially or in any other way.

LAMBERT: The scene in which Ruth goes to see the musical
comedy star, Hazel Dawn, to ask her advice about a theatrical
career—I'm sure that was cut. You must have shot it, you build up
to it, and then we never see it.

CUKOR: I think that was because it didn't turn out too well.
The actress didn't bring it off.

LAMBERT: And yet she's so good when you first see her in the opening sequence at the theater, singing and playing the violin at the same time.

CUKOR: The set was a reproduction of the original version of *Pink Lady*, which had been a great hit, and Hazel Dawn was a wonderful candy-box creature who did play the violin. (Very odd!) The choreography, and everything about the scene, was very authentic.

LAMBERT: And funny without poking fun.

CUKOR: Without patronizing. That's very important, it's the trick of doing period things without making them comic valentines. A lot of directors every time they show someone dancing the Charleston make the scene funny. But when you really look at them, the girls of that period were adorable. I suppose people who can't create the real thing have to make it ridiculous.

LAMBERT: The period quality in *The Actress* is very alive, except for one scene. When Ruth goes to the stage door of the theater, it looks like a conventional set—too dressed, and without atmosphere.

CUKOR: You're right, I'm afraid. We shot this in the studio, it was a short cut and we should have found the real thing. Real stage doors and alleys are always filthy and illogical and unexpected.

LAMBERT: The great triumph of the picture is Spencer Tracy. A beautifully written part, crusty and quirky on the outside and with a real tenderness inside. He's marvelous, so likable and maddening at the same time.

CUKOR: A part that's rare in modern comedy. You don't often get a part with that kind of richness for a great actor.

LAMBERT: I've left *Born Yesterday* until last, I suppose, because it's basically a very skillful adaptation of a Broadway hit and has a built-in success quality.

CUKOR: But that had its problems—of transferring a brilliant stage performance to a different medium, and of claustrophobia, because everything took place in one set. Garson solved that by moving the action around very convincingly without destroying the unity of the thing. It moved all over Washington and the Treasury Department, and Washington became a real dramatic personage in the story. I remember on location seeing the Jeffer-

Born Yesterday: Judy Holliday, Broderick Crawford. Compare
Jean Harlow and Wallace Beery in *Dinner at Eight*

son Memorial and being moved by it, and I said, "Let's photograph that." It wasn't just the physical photography of it, but something of the way I felt about it came across on the screen, I think. . . . Another problem was that there were things in the play that in those days were considered very censorable.

LAMBERT: Were they censored?

CUKOR: Yes. It seems ludicrous now, but twenty years ago you couldn't have a character say, "I love that broad," you couldn't even say "broad." And the nonsense that went on to get over the fact that Judy Holliday and Broderick Crawford were living together! It required the greatest skill and some new business that Garson invented, like Billie Dawn always creeping into the apartment the back way. We managed to make it amusing, I think, but it was so unnecessary. Still, we kept in a lot of the important things. For instance, Billie Dawn was a typically "fallen woman," she'd lived with this rich man for years. But at the end, when she fell in love with the young man and he kissed her, her reaction was absolutely virginal, as if she'd been kissed for the first time. The audience accepted that, it worked. But the idea that innocence could be born afresh in someone who was technically "fallen"—that was considered quite original and daring and romantic. This was a period when even a married couple on the screen had to sleep in twin beds. I had to deal with that in the wedding night scene in *The Marrying Kind*.

LAMBERT: The curse was taken off it there, I remember, because you set it up that the real furniture hasn't arrived in their apartment and they have to sleep on mattresses on the floor.

CUKOR: And Garson wrote in a rather charming line. Aldo Ray says wistfully to Judy Holliday, "Honey, couldn't we change the order to a double bed?" But then, of course, they get out of bed and immediately put on dressing gowns. Unbelievable today, when they'd be bare-assed from the start. But this was right at the end of that time when, if you committed adultery, you had to break a leg or be struck by lightning.

LAMBERT: Why didn't Garson take a script credit on *Born Yesterday*?

CUKOR: There was a situation. I'd signed to do the picture for Harry Cohn, and the first script in my opinion was no good and had thrown out some of the best things in Garson's play. I told Cohn I couldn't do it, and we reached the kind of compromise you often did with a tough showman like that. He'd paid a lot of money for the script and wouldn't spend any more, but he agreed that Garson could do a rewrite if he wasn't paid for it and didn't take a credit. (*Ironic*) These were the bad Hollywood days when everyone was supposed to be cynical and corrupt and you never lent yourself to a project just because you believed in it.

LAMBERT: I've left Judy Holliday until last, too, because this was her most famous role. Delicious though she is in the picture, her part in *The Marrying Kind* is richer, and I think of her first of all in that.

CUKOR: Like all the great clowns, Judy Holliday could also move you. She made you laugh, she was a supreme technician, and then suddenly you were touched. She could interpret a text with the subtlest detail, her pauses would give you every comma—

she'd even give the author a semicolon if he'd written one. And vocally she was fascinating, she had a way of hitting the note like a bull's-eye, and the slightest distortion in the recording meant that you lost something. If you lost any of the highs you lost a moment of comedy, and if you lost any of the lows you lost a moment of emotion. A true artist.

LAMBERT: Why did you stop working with the Kanins?

CUKOR: We were going to do another picture. Garson had a brilliant idea and wrote the opening of it. You were on a European train and you saw a lady in black sitting in one corner of a compartment, all alone. The camera moved very slowly up close to this lady—and it was Spence dressed as a widow. Then you discovered he was the head of a currency-smuggling gang based in Zurich. Spence was going to appear throughout the picture in different disguises. People in the State Department knew this chicanery was going on, and they got the best T-man from the Treasury—and it was Kate. She had this ruthless drive and purpose, and she was going to track him down and bring him to justice, like whoever-it-is pursues Valjean in *Les Miserables*. Then halfway through the picture she realizes she's stuck on him.

LAMBERT: Why didn't it go anywhere? Were you all going separate ways again by then?

CUKOR: I think so. And maybe Spencer felt they were getting too old to do this kind of film. He felt "a joke's a joke," and maybe he was right. Life changes. There's nothing worse than doing a certain kind of thing very charmingly and then running it into the ground.

LAMBERT: And in retrospect I wonder if they and you could ever have topped *Pat and Mike*. It's the summit of your whole collaboration.

CUKOR: We go over these things and I remember so much that I'd forgotten. With pleasure—and also some pardonable pride.

Interlude:
On Censorship and Eroticism

CUKOR: It's ludicrous when you look at it now, all the old nonsense about censorship, the rules about cleavage, mathematically calculated, and the length of the kiss. One rule that used to be followed very carefully was that if there was a kiss on a bed, one of the parties had to have their feet on the ground. Preposterous and unbelievable—but it led to something very curious. Because of the limitations, a special kind of eroticism was generated. To begin with, the actors and actresses themselves had to be very attractive. One of the great contributions of American pictures was the discovery of all these appetizing creatures, handsome men and beautiful girls. That was erotic to begin with. Then, they had to understand the rules, the language of the day. For example, if you read George Sand, which hardly anybody does anymore, her language may seem quite exaggerated, but it was very daring and passionate and explicit at the time. A friend of mine once told me, "You can only understand French acting if you live in France." In the same way, you have to read George Sand through

"Sometimes I think there was more sex within the Code than without it." Claire Bloom and Chad Everett in *The Chapman Report*

the eyes of the people living at that time. Then you realize she was the Jacqueline Susann of her day.

LAMBERT: But a Jacqueline Susann with class.

CUKOR: Yes. Her letters are most distinguished and charming. Anyway, in the days of censorship audiences got to understand the language of censorship and the reticence of it. You faded out on something quite innocent—Norma Shearer closes the door on Clark Gable—but the audience knew "that means they went to bed together."

LAMBERT: These devices were a legacy of Puritanism and nineteenth-century literature—seething passions underneath mounds of clothes. The kind of thing, in fact, that George Sand was reacting against.

CUKOR: Yes. And in films to generate that eroticism in the first place you had to get very attractive people, just as in nineteenth-century novels the heroes and heroines were usually described as very beautiful. Many of the girls in movies now are quite plain, and if they didn't strip to the buff it wouldn't work at all. It's a cheap cop-out to have unattractive people walking around naked, and there's very little skill or artistry involved in getting an unattractive nude couple into bed together. It seems passionless to me. When Clara Bow got out of bed, she looked all right, but when most girls do the same thing now, they look like hell. Sometimes I think there was more sex within the code than without it. Take that last picture of Antonioni's, *Zabriskie Point* —fifty couples screwing in the desert, and you couldn't care less.

Bhowani Junction
(1956)

L AMBERT: It's very sad that the studio recut *Bhowani Junction* so drastically. It's full of impressive things, things
unique in your work. The Indian atmosphere, the
handling of crowds, of people caught up in a huge
social crisis, the way you convey a country incessantly
on the move—

CUKOR: That's an impression I had in India—thousands of people swarming around, people, people, people! It was a different
kind of experience for me, it excited me—and then we had a bad
preview. In the story a Eurasian girl has affairs with three men.
Now that's not such a unique thing, but the audience seemed
unsympathetic to it, so the picture was not only recut but re-
arranged in a most uninteresting way.

LAMBERT: Including, I imagine, setting the story in flashback,
with the British colonel's voice over?

CUKOR: Yes. In the book I found something moving about the
girl's character. As an Anglo-Indian she's between two worlds, as
they say, and everything she does reflects this. She meets this
young Anglo-Indian and has an affair with him, then an Indian

Ava Gardner photographed by George Hoyningen-Huene

wants to marry her, and another tries to rape her, then she falls in love with the British colonel. . . . Well, in those days it seemed like too much promiscuity. Or maybe it wasn't played or written sympathetically enough to seem comprehensible to an audience.

LAMBERT: It seems totally comprehensible to me, and the way M-G-M fixed it up to "excuse" her behavior is maddening. All that insistence, in the colonel's narrative, about her dilemma as an Anglo-Indian—the point is made at least nineteen times. And there's a lot of other unnecessary exposition as well. I suppose they thought there were elements in the Indian situation, as well as the girl's situation, that an audience wouldn't understand. But you see the picture again now, and you dismiss in your mind all the added explanations, and it's clear you can take them out, take the whole flashback device out, and no one would be in the dark.

Bhowani Junction: Ava Gardner

CUKOR: There were other things cut, very daring things. The scene on the train with the British colonel—she realizes she's attracted to him and her behavior becomes rather loose and sluttish, she takes his toothbrush and cleans her teeth in front of him—

LAMBERT: Didn't she dip the brush in scotch first?

CUKOR: That, too, and all gone. The picture was seriously oversimplified and made to look sentimental at moments—which it never originally was. All the same, I thought Ava Gardner very attractive in the part.

LAMBERT: She's physically right to play an Anglo-Indian.

CUKOR: And the whole look of the production, if I may say so, was wonderful.

LAMBERT: It's dazzling. The color is unique, that use of a rather burnt-out, brownish tone all the way through—a nonrealistic touch that literally made you see India in a new light.

CUKOR: It was the way it looked to me. I was so aware of the unexpected things. You see the grandeur and the exposed electric wires at the same time. You see a great palace like the Taj Mahal and then suddenly a clothes tree and a Grand Rapids desk! All these things give an air of verisimilitude, of confusion, that is exciting. And technically it was a great challenge, you couldn't tell where the real interiors stopped and the studio sets began. Some of the interiors, and the railroad scenes, were shot in England. . . . (*Suddenly*) But there was this absolute *nonsense* that went on!

LAMBERT: (*rather startled*): Where?

CUKOR: In India! We wanted to do the whole thing there at first. But the whole Indian press was down on us, all the industry people there. We finally discovered it was because of one line in the script where the young Anglo-Indian says Nehru is a cunt, or a word to that effect. (*Amused*) Not Nehru, of course—I mean Gandhi. You explained to them, "But it's an unsympathetic character saying this." No good! There was a kind of maniacal, exasperating thing in their attitude. And then, in the scene where the passive resisters lie down in front of the train, we wanted to show the army pissing on them, pouring buckets of shit over them to make them get up. It used to happen, but they wouldn't let us do it. A great pity, that kind of emasculation. I saw so much that I couldn't use, and then they took out even more. . . . Now you could do it in a perfectly forthright way. The story is basically very serious and brutal, not romantic at all, and we had to lose so much of that because of censorship.

LAMBERT: The leading character in the film is really India, and it's even more censored than Ava Gardner. The character is still very powerful, but—

CUKOR (*emphatic*): It wasn't Amy Woodbridge, it wasn't "Pale Hands I Loved"! It was a real *look* at the place. We researched, we saw, and then we did it. There was so much you couldn't *help* catching just by looking! You couldn't go wrong. . . . But weren't the scenes of violence and riots still very good?

LAMBERT: The whole scene of the people lying down in front of the train, even though those buckets didn't have shit in them— just swill, I suppose—has a great impact.

CUKOR: There's really a lot that is very interesting, and it was a strenuous picture to make. . . . But some of the casting was wrong, too. Stewart Granger was wrong as the colonel.

LAMBERT: He's never struck me as much of an actor, although I thought he had a kind of natural pomposity that worked for the part.

CUKOR: I wanted Trevor Howard. Stewart Granger was just a movie star and he brought out the movie queen in Ava. She was good, but she and everything else would have been better with Trevor Howard. He'd have been more cruel, more real, in their whole affair. Several times in my life I've been defeated by certain casting things, and the script. . . . (*A smile*) I'm not always right, but when it goes wrong it's never my fault, you understand. This picture took a great deal of effort, a great deal of integrity and self-expression—all those qualities people bring up nowadays. We did it on location, we were clearly involved with a condition of the world, and a political struggle.

LAMBERT: The locations really drench the film in authenticity, and the incidental minor characters are equally authentic—but your three leading Indians are played by European actors. It shouldn't work, and yet it does.

CUKOR: Marne Maitland, who plays the peaceful revolutionary —not the extremist one—is half-Indian. The others are all English. That kind of thing *can* work and in this case it *had* to. I'll probably never get back to India, but we looked at a lot of Indian actors, and they were not so good, they were like Armenian opera

singers. I'm obviously burning my bridges, but that's the truth of it—and they might as well know. Indian actors are not so good.

LAMBERT: The one who plays Ranjit, the man she nearly marries, is particularly good.

CUKOR: Francis Matthews, yes, he's English, and doesn't he *look* right? If you know what you're doing you can get what you want. In a case like this the actor must have something right about him for starters. You can't take somebody blond and have him play an Indian, but if the coloring and the shape of the face and the manner seem right, then makeup and acting can bring it off. Otherwise, no amount of burnt cork is any good. But you never got the feeling of actors in burnt cork, did you?

LAMBERT: No. And in spite of everything that went wrong, I find *Bhowani Junction* one of your most personal and original films. It made me feel, too, what a pity it was you never made the film of *The Razor's Edge*.

CUKOR: Ah! I was going to. . . .

Passive resistance on the railroad tracks. Cukor rehearses a scene in *Bhowani Junction*. Above, Stewart Granger

Interlude:
On a Film That Never Was

CUKOR: Maugham's agent gave me the typescript of *The Razor's Edge* and said, "Willie's written this thing and wants you to read it." So I did and was very interested, and that same night I went to a party at Darryl Zanuck's. Orson Welles was there, talking to somebody. "I'm not really an educated man," I heard him say, "and I wish I were. I'd love to read *The Odyssey* in the original Greek and the Bible in the original Hebrew. . . ." I thought to myself, "That's strange, where have I heard someone say that before?" Then I remembered that I'd just read it, in *The Razor's Edge*! Larry, the leading character, says it. It struck me as very odd, since I was the only person in Hollywood who was supposed to have read it—the galleys weren't even out—and then it struck me as very funny because I discovered that Maugham's agent had saturated the market with copies of the typescript. Orson Welles had read it and been struck by it and was becoming the character, using some of his expressions. It's an indicative, interesting thing about him. Anyway, Zanuck bought the book and had a script written which I didn't like.

LAMBERT: The script they finally used, by Lamar Trotti?

CUKOR: Yes. So I said, "If you can get Maugham to do the script, I'd like to do the picture." Zanuck told me that Maugham was too busy and would cost too much extra money. So I called Willie in New York and he said, "I'll do it for nothing," which was all against the tradition that he was supposed to be very tight about money. So he came out here and stayed with me. He told Zanuck, "I'll start with page one and if you don't like it, you can chuck it into the wastepaper basket."

LAMBERT: How did the script turn out?

CUKOR: I thought it wonderful. He wrote a little prologue, giving advice to the actors and the director. I've got it here. (*Reads*) "Please note that this is, on the whole, a comedy and should be played lightly by everyone except in the definitely serious passages. The actors should pick up one another's cues as smartly as possible, and there's no harm if they cut in on one another as people do in ordinary life. I'm all against pauses and silences. If the actors cannot give significance to their lines without these, they're not worth their salaries. The lines are written to be spoken; they have all the significance needed if they are spoken with intelligence and feeling. The director is respectfully reminded that the action should accompany and illustrate the dialogue. Speed, speed, speed."

LAMBERT: I see the man of the theater rather than of the movies in some of that, but it's fascinating that Maugham saw *The Razor's Edge* as basically a comedy.

CUKOR: Well, the kind of script he wrote told the audience from the opening sequence, "This is the kind of picture it's going to be, you'd better listen, you listen here!" A taxi drives up to a house, a man gets out, he goes inside and immediately starts a long conversation with someone in the house. . . . The original script, you see, had what the studio called entertainment, which means dancing and country clubs and all that crap. Nothing to indicate you were supposed to sit down and listen to what was being said. Whatever important things this script retained were sandwiched between all kinds of nonsense.

LAMBERT: How did the studio react to Maugham's script?

CUKOR: Zanuck liked it very much, or said he did. But there were problems at the time—I was under contract to Metro, and Tyrone Power, whom they wanted for the lead, wasn't free. By

Somerset Maugham visits Cukor on the set (1959)

the time he became available I'd started a picture at Metro, and they went ahead with another director and also with the original script. (*A grimace*) More "entertainment." Willie behaved very well about it, considering he couldn't bear that script.

LAMBERT: It was a fascinating subject for a film, but what they turned out wasn't much good.

CUKOR: No, not good. But I don't see, all the same, how you could ever do the scene of the young man's "visions." Maugham didn't quite succeed with that in the novel, you know, the moment when the hero becomes a kind of saint.

LAMBERT: It's the kind of thing that's even harder to do in a film.

CUKOR: And they fell back on painted backdrops and sunsets, of course. Very few films about saintliness convince you. Bresson succeeds admirably in *The Diary of a Country Priest*.

LAMBERT: And Rossellini made a charming picture about Saint Francis.

CUKOR: I never saw that. But the moment of vision, hearing voices and all the rest of it, I wonder how you could do it.

LAMBERT: It's the same problem when films show you artists painting, writers sitting down to create a masterpiece—

CUKOR: Composers composing and certain actresses impersonating great dancers. . . . However, the whole *Razor's Edge* thing ended nicely in one way. The studio wanted to give Willie a present for having given them the script, so I suggested they buy him a painting, which they did. A Matisse, I think.

CUKOR: Maugham stayed with me while he wrote the screenplay of *The Razor's Edge*, and I was fascinated by his habits of work. He'd get up early in the morning, sit at a table in my guest room downstairs and write all morning in longhand. In the afternoon he'd read proofs or go out to the movies with Ethel Barrymore. And he was quite proud—that's what I remember next. When he showed me the script, all he said was, "It's antipragmatic writing."

LAMBERT: What did he mean by that?

CUKOR: I didn't know until years later, in England. Myself and Willie and the critic Desmond McCarthy were driving back to London from the country. They were playing a literary game, putting odds on which contemporary writers would survive. And Maugham said about himself, "I'm not a practicing writer." Then he explained, "I no longer write for profit." He'd made up his mind about that at the age of seventy-five, after all those years of working very hard and only undertaking things that would turn out profitably. Now it was different. He'd rather casually promise to select the ten greatest novels in the world and write a preface to each of them. He didn't realize at first what he'd let himself in for, but there were brilliant things in the prefaces. And then he'd agree to write some literary articles, one of them on Goethe. This meant rereading all of Goethe, which he'd read as a boy in German. Absolute hell! One of the things he gave up was writing fiction. And he said, "Not being a practicing writer, not being a creative writer anymore, is very lonely. Your characters don't exist with you anymore." I believe that explains partially why he

With the script that never was for a film that never was:
Maugham, Darryl Zanuck, Cukor

often seemed distracted in real life, he was always so involved with his characters. In his last years, when he wasn't always sure what was going on, I had lunch with him and Alan Searle, his secretary and companion for many years, in Venice. Willie began talking about an elderly couple in the restaurant, sketching a story about them, and Alan and I were distracted for a moment when a funeral procession passed along the Grand Canal. (It was a sight you couldn't help being distracted by, those black gondolas filled with people in black.) Willie got into a fury. "You fools," he said, "I'm giving you a *story*! And you're not *listening*!" You could see how the creative process was starving. . . .

LAMBERT: All the accounts of Maugham's last years sound terribly sad.

CUKOR: Yes, you felt they were a culmination of many struggles. He got very confused about time, you know, would drop off to sleep during the day and then become wide awake in the early hours of the morning, wanting to talk about all sorts of things, writing and money and people he had grudges against and planned to get even with. . . . But all his life he'd been nagged by ill-health and bad nerves and, as everyone knows, a stammer. He was always trying new things to relax himself, sports and Yoga and hypnotism, and finally those injections by a Swiss doctor that are supposed to stop you from aging.

LAMBERT: Do you think he was always an essentially lonely man?

CUKOR: Probably. In spite of his stammer he was a great talker and *raconteur*. He talked fascinatingly on a great variety of subjects—except himself. He once said to Alan Searle, "Never tell about your origins." So one never knew a great deal, except the outlines of what everyone knows. I would say that he had many pleasures but no real happiness.

LAMBERT: What were his pleasures?

CUKOR: Writing, of course—a pleasure and a passion as well as a discipline. It stimulated him to constant observation. He was endlessly curious about people and the world. It also brought him success, the fruits of which he openly enjoyed. One of his famous sayings was that "Money is the sixth sense that enables you to enjoy the other five." His beautiful house at Cap Ferrat meant a great deal to him. He read constantly, always rereading the classics and talking about them. He played a great deal of bridge. . . .

LAMBERT: And painting? He had this great collection.

CUKOR: Yes, but Alan Searle told me that Willie, in spite of his knowledge of art, never really cared for his pictures. It was Alan's pleasure in them that he cared about.

LAMBERT: In his book about Maugham, Garson Kanin quotes him as saying he felt *The Razor's Edge* was his last major work. When the movie was taken out of both your hands, how serious a blow do you suppose it was for him?

CUKOR: I'm sure he was deeply disappointed, more then he let on. But for all of his life no kind of disappointment or upset, personal or professional, could ever affect Willie's terrific determination to work, to go on producing what he wanted to produce. This was something that always impressed me about him. Work was his lifebelt, and he knew it, and he held onto it for as long as humanly possible. . . . We liked each other, I admired him very much, and the rest is a mystery. It couldn't be anything else. Here was a man who decided to write a book about his life as a writer and his experiences and in the first chapter of *The Summing Up* told you, "I have no desire to bare my heart." Willie said it, and that says it.

Heller in Pink Tights
(1960)

LAMBERT: This is quite a strange film, beautiful to look at, a new and very convincing feel of the West, and a script with abrupt switches of tone. A comedy or a drama?

CUKOR: A romantic comedy.

LAMBERT: And set up by Carlo Ponti as a vehicle for Sophia Loren?

CUKOR: With Paramount, yes. Truth to tell, there was never a story, but the *subject* attracted me. I'd always wanted to do a picture about a troupe of traveling actors and their adventures in the pioneer days. It always struck me as romantic and scary and authentically real. These actors, without in a sense being aware of it, were traveling in culture—they even brought it to California. They acted rather badly, but they did Shakespeare. In the retreat from Moscow, Napoleon had a troupe of comedians with him—there they were, in all that snow—and the idea of theatrical troupes venturing into territory like that has always fascinated me.

LAMBERT: It's the element of the film that comes through most strongly. You get this very special look at the West, seen through the eyes of actors at the time. And the color—

CUKOR (*eagerly*):—is ravishing! Beautiful, beautiful sets, too! It's the only Western I ever did, and when I saw the wagons crossing Arizona I was truly thrilled, the light is so wonderful there. I think you can see a lot of good documentation—the look of the Indians, the look of the frontier, the mud in the main street of the town. I like the theater scenes, too, the way those performances of *Mazeppa* and *La Belle Hélène* are re-created.

LAMBERT: All the detail is very creative and eye-catching. You showed some of the most convincing Indians I've ever seen, particularly in that moment when two of them first stumble on the troupe. They look so astonished and dowdy and alien, the opposite of conventional redskins.

CUKOR: They were taken from photographs. Part of their costumes were discarded Civil War uniforms. And they'd been hiding behind a rock—

LAMBERT: Yes, their costumes were camouflaged.

CUKOR: All these things were exact reproductions. When the troupe first arrives in the town and sees those dead Indians laid out on the boards, that was from photographs. And when the Indians attack the troupe and steal their costumes, that was based on something described by the traveling actor Joseph Jefferson in his autobiography. You see them finally caught and hanged, still wearing togas and Elizabethan ruffles—a good, funny scene.

LAMBERT: The interiors also have some beautiful color effects. That saloon bar with its very intense orange-red walls—

CUKOR: That was Gene Allen's idea. It's a beautiful moment when Sophia Loren walks into it, wearing white, with all the men in black.

LAMBERT: And I remember the set for her bedroom, the blue of the walls repeated in the fabric of her petticoat.

CUKOR: Something of a Renoir effect. . . . George Hoyningen-Huene created some brilliant costumes, especially for the theater scenes. He explored all the old wardrobe storage rooms at the studio and put together a mixture of costumes from different periods.

LAMBERT: Visually it's one of your most adventurous pic-

tures, and there are strange and funny episodes. It's a pity the script disintegrates completely at the end, which is just ordinary melodrama.

CUKOR: No real story there, as I said. But didn't you like some of the performances, too? I thought Sophia Loren very good, light and humorous.

LAMBERT: With a quality I've only seen in the best of her films directed by De Sica, the first one, *Gold of Naples*. She's not freaky and statuesque, but relaxed.

CUKOR: And you see her humor. She's really adorable.

LAMBERT: Not much charm or humor in her partner, Anthony Quinn, by the way.

CUKOR (*an emphatic nod of agreement*): But Eileen Heckart is a stage mother to end all stage mothers, and the daughter, what's her name—

LAMBERT: Margaret O'Brien. She makes a quite fiendish, sly ingénue.

CUKOR: She was our technical expert on certain things, because she was a famous child actress. She'd tell me, "When I'm having the row with my mother, I break off to smile very sweetly at anyone who passes, then go back to the row. . . ." She's a real movie actress, she looks at the dead bodies and you know they're dead, she feels cold and makes you feel the cold.

Heller in Pink Tights: Sophia Loren

My Fair Lady
(1964)

⌘

LAMBERT: Would you say that *My Fair Lady* was more prepackaged than most of your films?

CUKOR (*bristling slightly*): That's what you intellectuals are pleased to say.

LAMBERT: No. I'm not really an intellectual and it didn't please me to say it. I meant that Jack Warner, the producer, must have assembled the major creative elements in advance.

CUKOR: A lot of things are prepackaged. *Gone with the Wind* was the greatest prepackage of all. Anyway, people were very possessive about this one. "If you don't do it as well as it was done on the stage," they said, "we'll shoot you." But I somehow felt that I could. When Jack Warner asked me, "Would you like to do *My Fair Lady?*" I told him, "Yes, I think you've made a very intelligent choice." Of course, there were certain limitations from the start. Shaw's play had been an enormous success, and you couldn't change the text, his executors wouldn't allow it. (Not that I wanted to pull it apart at the seams.) My only criticism of what we did is that some of the choreography might have been bolder.

LAMBERT: Isn't it the only color film on which you didn't work with George Huene?

CUKOR: Yes, that was prepackaged, I admit—Cecil Beaton was one of the most important ingredients. He was engaged for the sets and costumes at the same time I was engaged as director. (*The shadow of a smile*) I know you're dying to have me go on about *that!*

LAMBERT: It's so unlike you to dry up. I'm quite disconcerted.

CUKOR (*a considerable pause*): As everyone knows, we didn't get on very well. I don't really understand why someone as talented as Beaton has to be so . . . (*reluctantly*) ungenerous. I suppose the fact that in picture making you're part of a team makes it difficult for him. He's a star performer in his own right, and very conscious of it and eager for publicity. In moviemaking you respect every contribution, but you have to work for the same aim, which is the director's aim.

LAMBERT: Is Beaton really more at home in the theater?

CUKOR: Perhaps. There's no doubt he was a great help to the art director, Gene Allen, with whom, as you know, I've worked very closely on many pictures.

LAMBERT: Was Gene Allen more responsible for the sets and Beaton for the costumes?

CUKOR: Not quite. . . . Beaton's a man of great taste and knowledge and an expert on the Edwardian period. However, his sets were technically very difficult to create, and Gene Allen certainly did the lion's share of the practical work, as well as a lot of designing. I think it would be fair to say that Gene executed the sets and made a very important contribution to the conception of them.

LAMBERT: The most brilliant thing in the picture is the Ascot sequence. Whose idea was it to stylize it so completely?

CUKOR: It was stylized on the stage.

LAMBERT: I know, but to carry that kind of stylization over to a movie was quite daring. I waited to see whether you'd bring on *real* horses, and how. The way they're preceded by a thunderous sound effect, and then pass very close to the camera—

CUKOR: There was really no other way we could have done it.

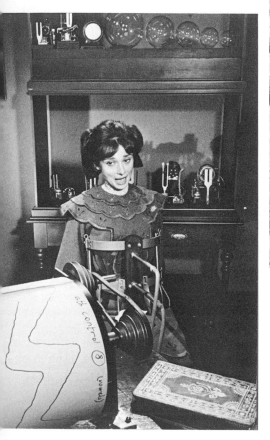

My Fair Lady: Three stages of
Eliza Doolittle (Audrey Hepburn)

"I think she's got it!" Rex Harrison, Audrey Hepburn,
Wilfrid Hyde-White in *My Fair Lady*

With Cecil Beaton on the set of *My Fair Lady*

There's a big number sung during the sequence, so it couldn't be realistic. Nor could the picture as a whole. It had to take place in a kind of dream world. You couldn't show the real Covent Garden, or the real Wimpole Street—you had to get the essence of things rather than the actuality. So in the Ascot sequence we gave an *effect* of horses, but we never cut away to the whole, realistic thing.

LAMBERT: Shavian comedy is larger than life, and I suppose this applies to the backgrounds as well as to the characters. The trouble with the movie of *Caesar and Cleopatra* was that it made the period sets literal and too solid, quite at variance with the way the characters behaved.

CUKOR: Yes, although we did a lot of research for the sets and the background, it was in order to *know* what we had to stylize. In England, Beaton, Gene Allen and I looked at actual houses to get the architectural feel. We'd go through book after book of the period and suddenly something would hit us. "Here's a significant detail," we'd say. "They'd have a gong in the hall." Little details like that bring places and habits to life, like the stuffed animals on the second floor of Professor Higgins' house and the *art nouveau* in his mother's house. Beaton was very good at that kind of thing. In the same way, we checked on all the techniques of phonetics. We discovered a man who'd been a pupil of Jones', the original of Shaw's Higgins. We made all the instruments he actually used, so all of that was correct.

LAMBERT: Had you seen the British film *Pygmalion?*

CUKOR: Oh, yes. Lerner and Loewe based their book for the stage musical on Shaw's screenplay for the British film. He wrote some new scenes for it and a new ending. We used even more of Shaw's screenplay than the stage version did. But the real difference between *My Fair Lady* on the stage and screen and *Pygmalion* on the screen and in most stage productions lay in the casting of Rex Harrison. Eliza was usually played by one of those overpowering actresses, and Higgins became an almost subsidiary, rather weak character. In the British film Leslie Howard did him charmingly as a romantic, but Rex hit the fanaticism, the possessed quality, and this made him infinitely touching and original. Also, he invented that unique musical parlando with people.

LAMBERT: Which has been much imitated.

CUKOR: Disastrously. Rex's performance, I think, is the most dazzling piece of work, even better on the screen than on the stage. We didn't postsync his numbers, by the way. Both of us felt they'd lose directness that way, so he wore a concealed mike. The result was that Rex said himself that certain laughs in the lyrics he could never get on the stage; he needed the intimacy of this technique with the camera for them.

LAMBERT: What about the casting of Audrey Hepburn? Was that Jack Warner's decision?

CUKOR: Yes. There was a great deal of controversy about Julie Andrews not getting it, I know. But I thought Audrey played it very charmingly. In the early scenes, maybe—

LAMBERT: She had problems there.

CUKOR: I think every actress has problems there.

LAMBERT: Not Wendy Hiller in the original film. Isn't it partly a question of suitability? Wendy Hiller had a kind of sturdy, earthy quality. You could accept her at once as a Cockney and a creature from the slums.

CUKOR: She's certainly a wonderful actress and gave the impression of great distinction in the later part, too. Still, I think we did the last scene better. There's a savagery in Shaw's directions which is usually omitted. He writes, "Eliza flings herself with a cry onto the hearthstone." He meant for her to have a real outburst here, to let off all the steam she'd stored up about Higgins' lack of appreciation for what she'd done. This didn't happen on the stage either. I went back to Shaw, and when Eliza throws the slippers at Higgins and rails at him, it's played all out. I thought Audrey did that very well. She looked exactly like Shaw's description of Eliza at that moment—"dangerously beautiful."

Interlude:
On Projects

LAMBERT: Apart from *The Razor's Edge* and that anti-Nazi story, *Escape*, that you wanted to do, what other projects have fallen through during your career?

CUKOR: There are so many. . . . Aldous Huxley was a great friend of mine and twice we nearly worked together. He was working at Metro on *Pride and Prejudice*, but it went another way and they gave it to another director. Aldous was a man of exceptional intelligence, erudition, humanity and humor, but I have to say that he wasn't a dramatist. In everything else he amazed me. When I was shooting *A Double Life*, I told him about the *Othello* scenes and he recommended some background music for them. He mentioned a French collection of music called, I believe, *Anthologie Sonore*, and said, "It contains some ceremonial music written for the doges." Sure enough it did, and we got it and used it.

LAMBERT: What was the second project?

CUKOR: He talked to me about the great Quaker woman Margery Fry. Kate Hepburn was going to play her. Aldous knew all about prison conditions in England in the early nineteenth century, how the male jailers were so frightened of the women prisoners—prostitutes waiting to be hanged or sent to Australia—they wouldn't dare enter their cages. Then this very quiet and gently bred woman would walk in among these desperate creatures and they loved her. . . . (*Laughs*) You think we could still do that with Elizabeth Taylor?

LAMBERT: You also had a plan, I think, to make *Far from the Madding Crowd* with Vivien Leigh.

CUKOR: Yes, about twenty years ago. I mentioned it to Maugham and he said, "Oh, I'm surprised!" I told him I'd been very moved by the novel, but he said, "*I* thought the characters were mere figments of a melodramatic imagination." So that was Willie Maugham on Thomas Hardy. I still thought it would make a bang-up picture, but for reasons I don't remember the project didn't work out with Vivien. We started it up again for Olivia de Havilland, but that didn't go either. Maybe I didn't push it hard enough, and maybe I was wrong about the material, because finally a very talented director made the picture and it didn't turn out so well.

LAMBERT: What about Romain Gary's novel *Lady L.*?

CUKOR: That story's like a mushroom, it has no roots. It's very diverting, of course. We never really got the right cast together, and Metro wanted to cast a lady who was absolutely wrong.

LAMBERT: Gina Lollobrigida. Is there anything you think she's right for?

CUKOR (*a smile but no answer*): I just walked out on that one, I got a doctor's certificate to say I was sick. I don't think Metro ever quite forgave me. They finally made the picture, with Sophia Loren, and I heard it was a disaster.

LAMBERT: There were other projects with Garbo, I believe.

CUKOR: Yes. *Sapho* by Daudet, a wonderful story. She'd made a silent version of it called *Love* or *Inspiration* or something. I wanted to do it again, with Montgomery Clift, and tried to get it off the ground several times, but it never worked. I'd still like to do it, maybe with Jeanne Moreau, but people say it's old-fashioned now. I don't think so. You just have to know how to do it, like *Little Women*.

LAMBERT: And *My Cousin Rachel*?

CUKOR: I was going to do that and spoke to Garbo about it, but

Aldous Huxley at Cukor's house

she didn't want to. I decided to go ahead anyway and went to England and talked with Daphne du Maurier. I learned a lot about Cornwall, and then I saw Richard Burton in a play, and I cabled Darryl Zanuck and said he should be engaged. But then I didn't agree with the script or the sets—the house looked like something out of *Peg O' My Heart*—and I withdrew. Zanuck cast Burton, though, and it began his American career.

LAMBERT: You once mentioned you were offered the Tennessee Williams play *Cat on a Hot Tin Roof.*

CUKOR: I turned it down because at that time it wasn't possible to deal honestly with the homosexuality. But a few years before that Kate Hepburn had a wonderful idea. Laurette Taylor was playing in New York in *The Glass Menagerie*, and Kate said, "Why don't we shoot a film of it there with Laurette, and myself as the crippled girl, and Spencer as the Gentleman Caller?" But

[248]

somebody else already had the rights, and we couldn't get them away. . . . I also turned down *Love Me or Leave Me*, the Ruth Etting story. It was going to be done with Ava Gardner, but I just didn't cotton to it. You know how I feel about gangsters. I never saw the picture they made, but I heard it was bang-up, and Ava said to me, "Well, we made a big mistake." And I told her, "Dear, if you and I had done it, it wouldn't have been as good." So there you are.

LAMBERT: And what happened to the Lesley Blanch story, *The Nine-Tiger Man?*

CUKOR: I still want to do that very much. The difficulty was, the budget came out at twelve million dollars. Quite unnecessary —it shouldn't be done in a big way. Fox wanted to find a star to play the Indian prince, but we couldn't, and they didn't want to invest all that money on a picture without names. But I haven't abandoned it. It's a charming story.

Justine
(1969)

LAMBERT: After the *Sylvia Scarlett* preview, Pandro Berman said he never wanted to see you again. How did you happen to be reunited with him on *Justine*?

CUKOR (*amused*): We'd been reunited years before on *Bhowani Junction*. He asked me to take over *Justine* after the company came back from the locations in Tunisia.

LAMBERT: So the location work is Joseph Strick's, who began directing the picture, and the studio sequences are all yours?

CUKOR: Yes. But the location stuff was not very selected and terribly antiseptic. The streets they photographed over there—there's no street in Beverly Hills that clean. A lot of it we couldn't use. If I'd been able to get a real crack at that, the whole picture would have smelled much more Mediterranean and Oriental. From stills they'd taken over there we did construct an Alexandria street in the studio, the one right outside the brothel. And we cast the street people here, Egyptians, Greeks, everybody —that's the great resource Hollywood has. The exteriors of Justine's country house were nice—they'd found a Turkish fort—but, unhappily, the choice of her town house was quite wrong. They used the D'Erlanger place in Tunis and the downstairs looked like an unsuccessful hotel. So we played most of the scenes upstairs, for which we furnished a quite different kind of set.

LAMBERT: In taking over the picture, you obviously went first for atmosphere, and I'm sure you were right. The script doesn't make sense, it seems to have had no idea of what kind of approach to take and how much of the Lawrence Durrell novels to use. The result is a bit like *Zaza*. I enjoyed the texture and the deliberate artifice and some of the acting, mainly Anna Karina and Dirk Bogarde.

CUKOR: Yes, but unfortunately I found some of the other players were quite inadequate for their parts. I took the picture on because I hadn't worked in some time, various projects had fallen through, and it was a professional challenge. I thought, "Yes, I can do this"—but had I known the full *horror* of some things. . . . (*A long sigh*) Of course, *she* was the great disaster.

LAMBERT: Anouk Aimee.

CUKOR: It was very disconcerting, the only time I've ever had anything to do with somebody who didn't try.

LAMBERT: A blank wall?

CUKOR: A blank, boring wall. She didn't try and she was indomitably refined—wouldn't do the coarseness of it. But Karina and Dirk and Philippe Noiret, they really lent themselves to it. But most of the others—that girl who played Dirk's blind sister—

LAMBERT: She'd been cast, too, before you took over?

CUKOR: Oh, yes. Oh, Christ.

LAMBERT: But I imagine you had full control over the sets.

CUKOR: And the costumes. Although *she* made trouble over *her* clothes.

LAMBERT: One of the best scenes is the masked costume ball. How much of that did Strick shoot?

CUKOR: A few pieces, and they looked like the waxworks.

LAMBERT: Some of the high-angle shots of all the dancers in the courtyard don't match the rest. Those must have been Strick's.

CUKOR: Yes. We couldn't afford to reshoot everything.

LAMBERT: It's still a quite compelling virtuoso sequence. And the opening of the picture is equally good—Karina dancing, then suddenly screaming and taking sick and running into the street—

CUKOR: A young Frenchman had been shooting a documentary

out there, and I was able to use some of his stuff. All the shots of people passing through the bazaars I glommed onto. And some of the dancing. (*Amused*) I have to say, some of what you see is really the greatest artistry. The agony of trying to create a child brothel! They didn't want the picture to get an X rating, so we had to work around all that. They brought me in the youngest-looking eighteen-year-olds they could find, but they looked like any other whores. I thought, now what the hell can I do? And somebody suggested midgets. So we used a lot of real children on the outside, inferring they were on the inside, too—but you only saw the midgets inside. How much more shocking if they'd all been real children. . . . In addition to everything else, we had censorship trying to cut the balls off the picture. And yet we got some startlingly good notices in New York.

Justine: Anouk Aimee, Michael York

LAMBERT: Vincent Canby in the New York *Times* seemed to understand what you were up to, the deliberate studio exoticism and all that.

CUKOR: Truth to tell, we should have gone to Alexandria and shot it there.

LAMBERT: Except that Alexandria is not the place it was when Durrell wrote about it.

CUKOR: I know, it looks like a lot of other places. The entrance to every city—London, Chicago—always looks the same now. And at the ocean they always have high-rise buildings. Still, you could go in there, with an eye, and redress and select.

LAMBERT: Or, on the other hand, do what you started to do. If it had been possible to use the studio technique consistently throughout, the way Von Sternberg used to—

CUKOR: I agree it was the only thing to try, under the circumstances. We did the best we could and we came up with some interesting things.

LAMBERT: And enough of them to make you see how completely fascinating the picture could have been.

Epilogue:
On Survival

CUKOR: In a long career, if a thing doesn't go, you must have the courage to say, "Well, it didn't go," and not think that your life was ruined. I've had three or four pictures almost wrecked by other people's cutting. I also shot a picture called *Desire Me* from a script that didn't really make sense, and when it was finished I was just removed from the picture, and another director reshot a good deal of it with the understanding that his name wouldn't appear on the credits. (Since very little of the final footage was mine, I wouldn't allow my name to be on the picture either. I think it was the only film released without a director's credit.) Then, of course, I was removed from *Gone with the Wind*. But I've never thought I was going to be exiled or buried. I just thought, "Well, so what?" All the same, you need a great deal of character to withstand the way you're treated sometimes. With a successful picture, you're good news. When you're not, people become rather offhand and casual. After I was taken off *Desire Me*, three colleagues came to visit me, and I said, "Now I know who'll come to my funeral." They were Margaret Booth, the head cutter at

The survivor, with Clark Gable during rehearsals
of *Gone with the Wind*

Metro, my old assistant, and the cameraman Joe Ruttenberg.
They were very sweet and tactful. "I can just see my own funeral," I said, "with only you three coming—and all those hollyhocks." There was a flower shop opposite Metro that seemed to
sell nothing except those poisonous pink hollyhocks, the great,
tall ones. That's how I imagined my funeral, those three friends
and a mass of pink hollyhocks. As Fannie Brice said, "The older
you get, the tougher it is to brush off them knocks." She was
right, but you have to brush them off. Whatever doubts may be
stirring inside you, you must say, "I've not gone mad since last
week, I'm still the same person." Don't let it damage you! It's not
easy, of course, and these days everyone's such a great expert they

write you off awful fast. (*Smiles*) But, of course, you can always turn into a very respected figure. There's this great new profession of film historians, and they're mostly young people, and they know everything, and they even praise your most disastrous films very highly. I'm very touched by their love of pictures. They ask me to lecture, but I refuse, because there's nothing more boring to me than to see someone get up on a platform and you think, "Holy Christ, he's going to talk. . . ."

LAMBERT: In a way, what you're saying is that the secret of survival is not to panic.

CUKOR: Not to panic and not to wilt. Certain people get dim when they grow older, they just seem to wilt and disappear. Just

as others start out with enormous promise and then seem to poop out. Is that lack of ambition or intelligence, or is it glandular? I think it's glandular. . . . Anyway, it's important not to panic or wilt and not to ape the times when you feel you're not part of them. Just try and understand them and continue to stand on your own feet.

Early days on *Gone with the Wind*: directing Clark Gable and Vivien Leigh, with Olivia de Havilland (left)

A Cukor Filmography

1930. GRUMPY. *Co-director:* Cyril Gardner. *Screenplay:* Doris Anderson, from a play by Horace Hodges and Thomas Wigney. *Photography:* David Abel. *Editor:* Cyril Gardner. *Cast:* Cyril Maude, Phillips Holmes, Paul Cavanagh, Paul Lukas, Frances Dade. (Paramount, 74 min.)

1930. THE VIRTUOUS SIN. *Co-director:* Louis Gasnier. *Screenplay:* Martin Brown and Louise Long, from a play by Lajos Tihaly. *Photography:* David Abel. *Cast:* Kay Francis, Walter Huston, Paul Cavanagh, Kenneth MacKenna. (Paramount, 80 min.)

1930. *THE ROYAL FAMILY OF BROADWAY. *Co-director:* Cyril Gardner. *Screenplay:* Herman J. Mankiewicz and Gertrude Purcell, from the play by Edna Ferber and George Kaufman. *Photography:* George Folsey. *Editor:* Edward Dmytryk. *Cast:* Ina Claire, Fredric March, Henrietta Crossman, Mary Brian, Charles Starrett. (Paramount, 82 min.)

1931. *TARNISHED LADY. *Screenplay:* Donald Ogden Stewart. *Photography:* Larry Williams. *Editor:* Barney Rogan. *Cast:*

* Discussed in the text.

Tallulah Bankhead, Clive Brook, Phoebe Foster, Alexander Kirkland, Osgood Perkins, Elizabeth Patterson. (Paramount, 85 min.)

1931. *GIRLS ABOUT TOWN. *Screenplay:* Raymond Griffith and Brian Marlow, from a story by Zoë Akins. *Photography:* Ernest Haller. *Cast:* Kay Francis, Joel McCrea, Lilyan Tashman, Eugene Pallette, Alan Dinehart, George Barbier, Louise Beavers, Lucille Webster Gleason. (Paramount, 90 min.)

1932. *WHAT PRICE HOLLYWOOD? *Producer:* David O. Selznick. *Screenplay:* Gene Fowler and Rowland Brown, from a story by Adela Rogers St. John. *Photography:* Charles Rosher. *Editor:* Jack Kitchen. *Sets:* Carroll Clark. *Music:* Max Steiner. *Cast:* Constance Bennett, Lowell Sherman, Neil Hamilton, Gregory Ratoff. (RKO-Radio, 87 min.)

1932. *A BILL OF DIVORCEMENT. *Producer:* David O. Selznick. *Screenplay:* Howard Estabrook and Harry Wagstaff Gribble, from the play by Clemence Dane. *Photography:* Sid Hickox. *Editor:* Arthur Roberts. *Sets:* Carroll Clark. *Music:* Max Steiner. *Cast:* Katharine Hepburn, John Barrymore, Billie Burke, David Manners, Henry Stephenson, Elizabeth Patterson, Bramwell Fletcher, Paul Cavanagh. (RKO-Radio, 80 min.)

1932. ROCKABYE. *Screenplay:* Jane Murfin and Kubec Glasmon, from the play by Lucia Bonder. *Photography:* Charles Rosher. *Editor:* George Hively. *Music:* Max Steiner. *Cast:* Constance Bennett, Joel McCrea, Paul Lukas, Walter Pidgeon, Jobyna Howland, Walter Catlett. (RKO-Radio, 70 min.)

1933. OUR BETTERS. *Producer:* David O. Selznick. *Screenplay:* Jane Murfin and Harry Wagstaff Gribble, from the play by Somerset Maugham. *Photography:* Charles Rosher. *Editor:* Jack Kitchen. *Music:* Max Steiner. *Technical Adviser:* Elsa Maxwell. *Cast:* Constance Bennett, Gilbert Roland, Charles Starrett, Anita Louise, Phoebe Foster, Grant Mitchell, Alan Mowbray, Violet Kemble Cooper, Minor Watson. (RKO-Radio, 85 min.)

1933. *DINNER AT EIGHT. *Producer:* David O. Selznick. *Screenplay:* Herman J. Mankiewicz and Frances Marion, from the play by Edna Ferber and George Kaufman. *Additional dialogue:* Donald Ogden Stewart. *Photography:* William Daniels. *Art directors:* Hobe Erwin and Van Nest Polglase. *Costumes: Costumes:* Adrian. *Cast:* Marie Dressler, John Barrymore, Wallace Beery, Jean Harlow, Lionel Barrymore, Billie Burke, Lee

Tracy, Madge Evans, Jean Hersholt, Karen Morley, May Robson, Phoebe Foster, Grant Mitchell, Elizabeth Patterson, Phillips Holmes. (M-G-M, 110 min.)

1933. *LITTLE WOMEN. *Producer:* David O. Selznick. *Screenplay:* Sarah Y. Mason and Victor Heerman, from the novel by Louisa M. Alcott. *Photography:* Henry Gerrard. *Editor:* Jack Kitchen. *Art directors:* Hobe Erwin and Van Nest Polglase. *Costumes:* Walter Plunkett. *Music:* Max Steiner. *Cast:* Katharine Hepburn, Joan Bennett, Paul Lukas, Frances Dee, Jean Parker, Edna May Oliver, Spring Byington, Douglass Montgomery, Henry Stephenson. (RKO-Radio, 117 min.)

1935. *DAVID COPPERFIELD. *Producer:* David O. Selznick. *Screenplay:* Howard Estabrook. *Adaptation:* Hugh Walpole, from the novel by Charles Dickens. *Photography:* Oliver T. Marsh. *Editor:* Robert J. Kern. *Art directors:* Cedric Gibbons, Merrill Pye and Edwin B. Willis. *Costumes:* Dolly Tree. *Special effects:* Slavko Vorkapich. *Music:* Herbert Stothart. *Cast:* Freddie Bartholomew, W. C. Fields, Lionel Barrymore, Maureen O'Sullivan, Madge Evans, Edna May Oliver, Lewis Stone, Frank Lawton, Elizabeth Allan, Roland Young, Basil Rathbone, Elsa Lanchester, Violet Kemble Cooper, Lennox Pawle, Jean Cadell, Jessie Ralph, Una O'Connor, Hugh Williams, Herbert Mundin, Hugh Walpole. (M-G-M, 135 min.)

1935. *SYLVIA SCARLETT. *Producer:* Pandro S. Berman. *Screenplay:* John Collier, Gladys Young and Mortimer Offner, from the novel by Compton Mackenzie. *Photography:* Joseph August. *Editor:* Jane Loring. *Art director:* Van Nest Polglase. *Music:* Roy Hunt. *Cast:* Katharine Hepburn, Cary Grant, Brian Aherne, Edmund Gwenn, Natalie Paley, Dennie Moore. (RKO-Radio, 90 min.)

1936. *ROMEO AND JULIET. *Producer:* Irving G. Thalberg. *Screen adaptation:* Talbot Jennings, from the play by Shakespeare. *Photography:* William Daniels. *Editor:* Margaret Booth. *Art director:* Cedric Gibbons. *Settings:* Oliver Messel and Cedric Gibbons. *Costumes:* Oliver Messel and Adrian. *Dance director:* Agnes de Mille. *Music:* Herbert Stothart. *Cast:* Norma Shearer, Leslie Howard, John Barrymore, Edna May Oliver, Basil Rathbone, C. Aubrey Smith, Andy Devine, Reginald Denny, Ralph Forbes, Conway Tearle, Violet Kemble Cooper, Henry Kolker, Robert Warwick. (M-G-M, 140 min.)

1936. *CAMILLE. *Producer:* Irving G. Thalberg. *Associate producer:* David Lewis. *Screenplay:* Zoë Akins, Frances Marion and James Hilton, from the play by Alexandre Dumas. *Photography:* William Daniels and Karl Freund. *Editor:* Margaret Booth. *Art director:* Cedric Gibbons. *Costumes:* Adrian. *Music:* Herbert Stothart. *Cast:* Greta Garbo, Robert Taylor, Lionel Barrymore, Henry Daniell, Elizabeth Allan, Laura Hope Crews, Lenore Ulric, Rex O'Malley, Jessie Ralph, E. E. Clive. (M-G-M, 108 min.)

1938. *HOLIDAY. *Producer:* Everett Riskin. *Screenplay:* Donald Ogden Stewart and Sidney Buchman, from the play by Philip Barry. *Photography:* Franz Planer. *Editors:* Otto Meyer and Al Clark. *Art directors:* Stephen Gooson and Lionel Banks. *Musical director:* Morris Stoloff. *Cast:* Katharine Hepburn, Cary Grant, Doris Nolan, Lew Ayres, Edward Everett Horton, Jean Dixon, Henry Kolker, Binnie Barnes, Henry Daniell. (Columbia, 93 min.)

1938. *ZAZA. *Producer:* Albert Lewin. *Screenplay:* Zoë Akins, from the play by Pierre Berton and Charles Simon. *Photography:* Charles Lang, Jr. *Editor:* Edward Dmytryk. *Art directors:* Hans Dreier, Robert Usher. *Costumes:* Edith Head. *Dance director:* LeRoy Prinz. *Songs:* Frederick Hollander and Frank Loesser. *Cast:* Claudette Colbert, Herbert Marshall, Bert Lahr, Helen Westley, Constance Collier, Genevieve Tobin, Walter Catlett, Rex O'Malley. (Paramount, 80 min.)

1939. *THE WOMEN. *Producer:* Hunt Stromberg. *Screenplay:* Anita Loos and Jane Murfin, from the play by Clare Boothe. *Photography:* Oliver T. Marsh and Joseph Ruttenberg. *Editor:* Robert J. Kern. *Art directors:* Cedric Gibbons and Wade B. Rubottom. *Sets:* Edwin B. Willis. *Costumes:* Adrian. *Music:* Edward Ward and David Snell. *Cast:* Norma Shearer, Joan Crawford, Rosalind Russell, Mary Boland, Paulette Goddard, Joan Fontaine, Lucile Watson, Phyllis Povah, Ruth Hussey, Virginia Weidler, Florence Nash, Margaret Dumont, Dennie Moore, Marjorie Main, Hedda Hopper. (M-G-M, 134 min.)

1940. *SUSAN AND GOD. *Producer:* Hunt Stromberg. *Screenplay:* Anita Loos, from the play by Rachel Crothers. *Photography:* Robert Planck. *Editor:* William H. Terhune. *Art directors:* Cedric Gibbons and Randall Duell. *Costumes:* Adrian. *Music:* Herbert Stothart. *Cast:* Joan Crawford, Melvyn Douglas, Rita Hayworth, John Carroll, Ruth Hussey, Nigel Bruce, Bruce

Cabot, Rose Hobart, Constance Collier, Marjorie Main, Dan Dailey, Gloria de Haven. (M-G-M, 115 min.)

1940. *THE PHILADELPHIA STORY. *Producer:* Joseph L. Mankiewicz. *Screenplay:* Donald Ogden Stewart, from the play by Philip Barry. *Photography:* Joseph Ruttenberg. *Editor:* Frank Sullivan. *Art directors:* Cedric Gibbons and Wade B. Rubottom. *Sets:* Edwin B. Willis. *Costumes:* Adrian. *Music:* Franz Waxman. *Cast:* Katharine Hepburn, Cary Grant, James Stewart, Ruth Hussey, John Howard, Roland Young, John Halliday, Mary Nash, Virginia Weidler, Henry Daniell. (M-G-M, 111 min.)

1941. *A WOMAN'S FACE. *Producer:* Victor Saville. *Screenplay:* Donald Ogden Stewart and Elliot Paul, from a play by Francis de Croisset, *Il était une fois. Photography:* Robert Planck. *Editor:* Frank Sullivan. *Art directors:* Cedric Gibbons and Wade B. Rubottom. *Sets:* Edwin B. Willis. *Costumes:* Adrian. *Music:* Bronislau Kaper. *Cast:* Joan Crawford, Melvyn Douglas, Conrad Veidt, Osa Massen, Reginald Owen, Albert Basserman, Donald Meek, Connie Gilchrist, Marjorie Main, Henry Daniell, Richard Nichols. (M-G-M, 105 min.)

1941. *TWO-FACED WOMAN. *Producer:* Gottfried Reinhardt. *Screenplay:* S. N. Behrman, Salka Viertel and George Oppenheimer, from a play by Ludwig Fulda. *Photography:* Joseph Ruttenberg. *Editor:* George Boemler. *Art directors:* Cedric Gibbons and Daniel B. Cathcart. *Costumes:* Adrian. *Special effects:* Warren Newcombe. *Hair styles:* Sydney Guilaroff. *Dance director:* Robert Alton. *Music:* Bronislau Kaper. *Cast:* Greta Garbo, Melvyn Douglas, Constance Bennett, Roland Young, Ruth Gordon, Robert Sterling, Frances Carson, Connie Gilchrist. (M-G-M, 95 min.)

1942. *HER CARDBOARD LOVER. *Producer:* J. Walter Ruben. *Screenplay:* John Collier, Jacques Deval, Anthony Veiller and William H. Wright, from the play by Jacques Deval. *Photography:* Harry Stradling and Robert Planck. *Editor:* Robert J. Kern. *Art directors:* Cedric Gibbons and Randall Duell. *Set decorator:* Edwin B. Willis. *Costumes:* Kalloch. *Music:* Franz Waxman. *Song,* "I Dare You": Burton Lane and Ralph Freed. *Cast:* Norma Shearer, Robert Taylor, George Sanders, Frank McHugh, Elizabeth Patterson, Chill Wills. (M-G-M, 90 min.)

1942. *KEEPER OF THE FLAME. *Producer:* Victor Saville. *Screen-*

play: Donald Ogden Stewart, from the novel by I. A. R. Wylie. *Photography:* William Daniels. *Editor:* James E. Newcombe. *Art directors:* Cedric Gibbons and Lyle Wheeler. *Sets:* Edwin B. Willis and Jack Moore. *Special effects:* Warren Newcombe. *Costumes:* Adrian. *Music:* Bronislau Kaper. *Cast:* Spencer Tracy, Katharine Hepburn, Richard Whorf, Forrest Tucker, Audrey Christie, Horace McNalley, Margaret Wycherly, Frank Craven, Percy Kilbride, Darryl Hickman. (M-G-M, 100 min.)

1944. *GASLIGHT. *Producer:* Arthur Hornblow, Jr. *Screenplay:* John van Druten, John L. Balderston and Walter Reisch, from the play by Patrick Hamilton. *Photography:* Joseph Ruttenberg. *Editor:* Ralph E. Winters. *Sets:* Paul Huldchinsky and Edwin B. Willis. *Art directors:* Cedric Gibbons and William Ferrari. *Special effects:* Warren Newcombe. *Costumes:* Irene, assisted by Marion Herwood. *Music:* Bronislau Kaper. *Cast:* Ingrid Bergman, Charles Boyer, Joseph Cotten, Angela Lansbury, Dame May Whitty, Barbara Everest, Emil Rameau, Eustace Wyatt, Halliwell Hobbes, Heather Thatcher, Charles Grossmith. (M-G-M, 114 min.)

1944. WINGED VICTORY. *Producer:* Darryl F. Zanuck. *Screenplay:* Moss Hart, from his own play. *Photography:* Glen MacWilliams. *Editor:* Barbara McLean. *Production design:* Harry Horner. *Art directors:* Lyle Wheeler and Lewis Creber. *Costumes:* Kay Nelson. *Special effects:* Fred Sersen. *Music:* David Rose. *Cast:* Lon McCallister, Jeanne Crain, Edmond O'Brien, Jane Ball, Mark Daniels, Don Taylor, Judy Holliday, Jo-Carroll Dennison, Lee J. Cobb, Peter Lind Hayes, Red Buttons, Barry Nelson, Gary Merrill. (Twentieth Century-Fox, 110 min.)

1947. *A DOUBLE LIFE. *Producer:* Michael Kanin. *Screenplay:* Ruth Gordon and Garson Kanin. *Photography:* Milton Krasner. *Editor:* Robert Parrish. *Art directors:* Bernard Herzbrun and Harvey Gillett. *Costumes:* Travis Banton and Yvonne Wood. *Special effects:* David S. Horsley. *Music:* Miklos Rosza. *Cast:* Ronald Colman, Signe Hasso, Edmond O'Brien, Shelley Winters, Millard Mitchell, Ray Collins, Philip Loeb, Whit Bissell, Charles La Torre, Joe Sawyer, Betsy Blair. (Universal-International, 103 min.)

1948. EDWARD, MY SON. *Producer:* Edwin H. Knopf. *Screenplay:* Donald Ogden Stewart, from the play by Noel Langley and Robert Morley. *Photography:* F. A. Young. *Editor:* Raymond Poulton. *Art director:* Alfred Junge. *Music:* John Woodridge.

Cast: Spencer Tracy, Deborah Kerr, Ian Hunter, Leueen Mac-Grath, James Donald, Mervyn Johns, Felix Aylmer. (M-G-M, 112 min.)

1949. *ADAM'S RIB. *Producer:* Lawrence Weingarten. *Screenplay:* Ruth Gordon and Garson Kanin. *Photography:* George J. Folsey. *Editor:* George Boemler. *Art directors:* Cedric Gibbons and William Ferrari. *Set decorators:* Edwin B. Willis, Henry W. Grace. *Costumes:* Walter Plunkett. *Special effects:* A. Arnold Gillespie. *Song,* "Farewell, Amanda": Cole Porter. *Music:* Miklos Rosza. *Cast:* Spencer Tracy, Katharine Hepburn, Judy Holliday, David Wayne, Tom Ewell, Jean Hagen, Hope Emerson, Eve March, Clarence Kolb. (M-G-M, 102 min.)

1950. A LIFE OF HER OWN. *Producer:* Voldemar Vetluguin. *Screenplay:* Isobel Lennart. *Photography:* George J. Folsey. *Editor:* George White. *Art directors:* Cedric Gibbons and Arthur Lonergan. *Set decorators:* Edwin B. Willis and Henry W. Grace. *Music:* Bronislau Kaper. *Cast:* Lana Turner, Ray Milland, Ann Dvorak, Louis Calhern, Tom Ewell, Barry Sullivan, Margaret Phillips, Jean Hagen. (M-G-M, 108 min.)

1950. *BORN YESTERDAY. *Producer:* S. Sylvan Simon. *Screenplay:* Albert Mannheimer (and Garson Kanin, uncredited), from the play by Garson Kanin. *Photography:* Joseph Walker. *Production design:* Harry Horner. *Editor:* Charles Nelson. *Music:* Frederick Hollander. *Cast:* Judy Holliday, Broderick Crawford, William Holden, Howard St. John, Frank Otto, Larry Oliver, Barbara Brown. (Columbia, 102 min.)

1951. THE MODEL AND THE MARRIAGE BROKER. *Producer:* Charles Brackett. *Screenplay:* Charles Brackett, Walter Reisch and Richard Breen. *Photography:* Milton Krasner. *Editor:* Robert Simpson. *Art directors:* Lyle Wheeler, John de Cuir. *Set decorators:* Thomas Little, Walter M. Scott. *Costumes:* Renie. *Music:* Cyril Mockridge. *Cast:* Jeanne Crain, Scott Brady, Thelma Ritter, Zero Mostel, Michael O'Shea, Helen Ford, Dennie Moore, Frank Fontaine. (Twentieth Century-Fox, 103 min.)

1951. *THE MARRYING KIND. *Producer:* Bert Granet. *Screenplay:* Ruth Gordon and Garson Kanin. *Photography:* Joseph Walker. *Editor:* Charles Nelson. *Art director:* John Meehan. *Set decorator:* William Kiernan. *Costumes:* Jean Louis. *Music:* Hugo Friedhofer. *Cast:* Judy Holliday, Aldo Ray, Madge Kennedy,

Sheila Bond, John Alexander, Phyllis Povah, Rex Williams, Peggy Cass, Mickey Shaughnessy. (Columbia, 108 min.)

1952. *PAT AND MIKE. *Producer:* Lawrence Weingarten. *Screenplay:* Ruth Gordon and Garson Kanin. *Photography:* William Daniels. *Art directors:* Cedric Gibbons and Urie McCleary. *Set decorators:* Edwin B. Willis, Hugh Hunt. *Special effects:* Warren Newcombe. *Katharine Hepburn's costumes:* Orry-Kelly. *Editor:* George Boemler. *Music:* David Raksin. *Cast:* Spencer Tracy, Katharine Hepburn, Aldo Ray, William Ching, Sammy White, George Matthews, Loring Smith, Phyllis Povah, Jim Backus, Chuck Connors. (M-G-M, 95 min.)

1953. *THE ACTRESS. *Producer:* Lawrence Weingarten. *Screenplay:* Ruth Gordon, from her play *Years Ago*. *Photography:* Harold Rosson. *Editor:* George Boemler. *Art directors:* Cedric Gibbons and Arthur Lonergan. *Set decorators:* Edwin B. Willis and Emile Kuri. *Costumes:* Walter Plunkett. *Special effects:* Warren Newcombe. *Musical director:* Bronislau Kaper. *Cast:* Jean Simmons, Spencer Tracy, Teresa Wright, Anthony Perkins, Ian Wolfe, Kay Williams, Mary Wickes. (M-G-M, 90 min.)

1954. *IT SHOULD HAPPEN TO YOU. *Producer:* Fred Kohlmar. *Screenplay:* Garson Kanin. *Photography:* Charles Lang. *Editor:* Charles Nelson. *Art director:* John Meehan. *Set decorator:* William Kiernan. *Costumes:* Jean Louis. *Music:* Frederick Hollander. *Cast:* Judy Holliday, Jack Lemmon, Peter Lawford, Michael O'Shea, Vaughn Taylor, Connie Gilchrist, Whit Bissel, Walter Klavun and (*TV panelists*) Constance Bennett, Ilka Chase, Wendy Barrie, Melville Cooper. (Columbia, 100 min.)

1954. *A STAR IS BORN. *Producer:* Sidney Luft. *Screenplay:* Moss Hart, based on the screenplay by Dorothy Parker, Alan Campbell and Robert Carson, based on the story by William A. Wellman and Robert Carson. *Photography* (Technicolor and CinemaScope): Sam Leavitt. *Special color adviser:* George Hoyningen-Huene. *Editor:* Folmar Blangsted. *Art director:* Malcolm Bert. *Set decorator:* George James Hopkins. *Costumes:* Jean Louis and Mary Ann Nyberg. *Art direction and costumes for "Born in a Trunk":* Irene Sharaff. *Production design:* Gene Allen. *Dance director:* Richard Barstow. *New songs:* Harold Arlen and Ira Gershwin. *"Born in a Trunk":* Leonard Gershe. *Musical director:* Ray Heindorf. *Cast:* Judy Garland, James Mason, Jack Carson, Charles Bickford, Tom

Noonan, Lucy Marlow, Amanda Blake, Irving Bacon. (Warner Brothers, 182 min., cut to 140 min.)

1956. *BHOWANI JUNCTION. *Producer:* Pandro S. Berman. *Screenplay:* Sonya Levien and Ivan Moffat, from the novel by John Masters. *Photography:* F. A. Young. *Special color consultant:* George Hoyningen-Huene. (CinemaScope, Eastmancolor.) *Art directors:* Gene Allen, John Howell. *Editors:* Frank Clarke, George Boemler. *Music:* Bronislau Kaper. *Cast:* Ava Gardner, Stewart Granger, Bill Travers, Abraham Sofaer, Francis Matthews, Marne Maitland, Peter Illing, Edward Chapman, Freda Jackson, Lionel Jeffries. (M-G-M, 109 min.)

1957. LES GIRLS. *Producer:* Sol C. Siegel. *Screenplay:* John Patrick, from a story by Vera Caspary. *Photography* (CinemaScope and Metrocolor): Robert Surtees. *Color coordinator:* George Hoyningen-Huene. *Editor:* Ferris Webster. *Art directors:* William A. Horning and Gene Allen. *Set decorators:* Edwin B. Willis and Richard Pefferle. *Costumes:* Orry Kelly. *Choreography:* Jack Cole. *Music and lyrics:* Cole Porter. *Musical director:* Adolph Deutsch. *Cast:* Gene Kelly, Mitzi Gaynor, Kay Kendall, Taina Elg, Jacques Bergerac, Leslie Phillips, Henry Daniell, Patrick Macnee. (M-G-M, 114 min.)

1957. WILD IS THE WIND. *Producer:* Hal Wallis. *Screenplay:* Arnold Schulman, from a story by Vittorio Nino Novarese. *Photography:* Charles Lang. *Editor:* Warren Low. *Art directors:* Hal Pereira, Tambi Larsen. *Set decorators:* Sam Cromer and Arthur Krams. *Costumes:* Edith Head. *Music:* Dmitri Tiomkin. *Cast:* Anna Magnani, Anthony Quinn, Anthony Franciosa, Dolores Hart, Joseph Calleia, Lily Valenty. (Paramount, 110 min.)

1960. *HELLER IN PINK TIGHTS. *Producers:* Carlo Ponti and Marcello Girosi. *Screenplay:* Dudley Nichols and Walter Bernstein, from a story by Louis L'Amour. *Photography* (Technicolor): Harold Lipstein. *Special color consultant:* George Hoyningen-Huene. *Editor:* Howard Smith. *Art directors:* Hal Pereira and Gene Allen. *Set decorators:* Sam Comer and Grace Gregory. *Choreography:* Val Raset. *Music:* Daniele Amfitheatrof. *Cast:* Sophia Loren, Anthony Quinn, Margaret O'Brien, Steve Forrest, Eileen Heckart, Ramon Novarro, Edmund Lowe, George Matthews, Edward Binns, Frank Silvera. (Paramount, 100 min.)

1960. LET'S MAKE LOVE. *Producer:* Jerry Wald. *Screenplay:* Norman Krasna. *Additional material:* Hal Kanter. *Photography* (De Luxe Color and CinemaScope): Daniel L. Fapp. *Color coordinator:* George Hoyningen-Huene. *Editor:* David Bretherton. *Art directors:* Lyle B. Wheeler and Gene Allen. *Set decorators:* Walter M. Scott and Fred M. Maclean. *Costumes:* Dorothy Jeakins. *Songs:* Sammy Cahn and James van Heusen. *Music:* Lionel Newman. *Cast:* Marilyn Monroe, Yves Montand, Tony Randall, Frankie Vaughan, Wilfrid Hyde-White, David Burns, Michael David, Madge Kennedy, Mara Lynn. (Twentieth Century-Fox, 119 min.)

1962. *THE CHAPMAN REPORT. A Darryl F. Zanuck Production. *Producer:* Richard D. Zanuck. *Screenplay:* Wyatt Cooper and Don M. Mankiewicz, from the novel by Irving Wallace. *Adaptation:* Grant Stuart and Gene Allen. *Photography* (Technicolor): Harold Lipstein. *Color coordination and titles:* George Hoyningen-Huene. *Editor:* Robert Simpson. *Production design:* Gene Allen. *Set decorator:* George James Hopkins. *Costumes:* Orry Kelly. *Music:* Leonard Rosenman. *Cast:* Jane Fonda, Shelley Winters, Claire Bloom, Efrem Zimbalist, Jr., Glynis Johns, Ray Danton, Ty Hardin, Andrew Duggan, John Dehner, Harold J. Stone, Corey Allen, Jennifer Howard, Chad Everett, Henry Daniell, Cloris Leachman. (Warner Brothers, 125 min.)

1964. *MY FAIR LADY. *Producer:* Jack L. Warner. *Screenplay, book and lyrics:* Alan Jay Lerner, from his stage play, based on *Pygmalion* by Bernard Shaw. *Photography* (Technicolor, Super-Panavision): Harry Stradling. *Production design, scenery and costumes:* Cecil Beaton. *Art director:* Gene Allen. *Editor:* William Ziegler. *Choreography:* Hermes Pan. *Music:* Frederick Loewe. *Music supervision:* Andre Previn. *Cast:* Audrey Hepburn, Rex Harrison, Stanley Holloway, Wilfrid Hyde-White, Gladys Cooper, Jeremy Brett, Theodore Bikel, Mona Washbourne, Isobel Elsom, John Holland, Henry Daniell, Veronica Rothschild. (Warner Brothers, 170 min.)

1969. *JUSTINE. *Producer:* Pandro S. Berman. *Screenplay:* Lawrence B. Marcus, from the *Alexandria Quartet* by Lawrence Durrell. *Photography:* (Panavision and De Luxe Color) Leon Shamroy. *Editor:* Rita Roland. *Art directors:* Jack Martin Smith, William Creber, Fred Harpman. *Set decorators:* Walter M. Scott, Ralph Bretton. *Costumes:* Irene Sharaff. *Choreography:* Gemze de Lappe. *Music:* Jerry Goldsmith. *Cast:* Anouk Aimee, Dirk

Bogarde, Anna Karina, Robert Forster, Michael York, Philippe
Noiret, John Vernon, Jack Albertson, Cliff Gorman, George
Baker, Elaine Church, Marcel Dalio, Michael Dunn, Barry
Morse. (Twentieth Century-Fox, 116 min.)

WORK IN PROGRESS

1972. TRAVELS WITH MY AUNT. *Producer:* Robert Fryer.
Screenplay: Hugh Wheeler and Jay Presson Allen, from the
novel by Graham Greene. With Katharine Hepburn. (M-G-M)

IN THE MARGIN

1929. *Dialogue director on *River of Romance*, based on Booth Tarkington's *Magnolia*, directed by Richard Wallace, with Buddy
Rogers, Henry B. Walthall and Mary Brian.

1930. *Dialogue director on *All Quiet on the Western Front*, from
the novel by Erich Maria Remarque, directed by Lewis Milestone, with Louis Wolheim and Lew Ayres.

1932. *Began directing *One Hour with You*, from Lubitsch's script,
but was removed after two weeks of shooting. Lubitsch took
over, but Cukor remained as his assistant. The credits read:
"Directed by Ernst Lubitsch, Dialogue Director, George
Cukor."

1939. *Spent several months on preparation of *Gone with the Wind*,
with David O. Selznick, and shot Vivien Leigh's test. Began
directing the film, but after three weeks of shooting Selznick
replaced him with Victor Fleming.

1943. In U.S. armed services. Produced a training film, *Resistance
and Ohm's Law*, for the U.S. Signal Corps.

1946. *Directed *Desire Me* for M-G-M, which was extensively reshot
by Mervyn Leroy. With Greer Garson and Robert Mitchum.
Cukor disowns the film.

1959. Took over *Song Without End* for Columbia when Charles
Vidor died after a month of shooting. A biography of Franz
Liszt, with Dirk Bogarde, Capucine and Ivan Desny. Cukor
asked that Charles Vidor receive sole credit.

1962. Began shooting *Something's Got to Give* for Twentieth
Century-Fox, with Marilyn Monroe, Dean Martin, Phil Silvers
and Cyd Charisse. The film was abandoned after three weeks

of shooting, owing to Marilyn Monroe's nonappearance on the set. She died shortly after the film was closed down.

THEATER

During the twenties, in Rochester, New York, and New York City, Cukor directed a number of plays, including:

THE GREAT GATSBY. With James Rennie, Florence Eldridge, Elliot Cabot.

THE CONSTANT WIFE. With Ethel Barrymore.

*HER CARDBOARD LOVER. With Laurette Taylor, Leslie Howard.

THE DARK. With Louis Calhern, Ann Andrews.

*THE FURIES. With Laurette Taylor, Alan Campbell, Estelle Winwood.

A FREE SOUL. With Kay Johnson, Lester Lonergan, Melvyn Douglas.

YOUNG LOVE. With Dorothy Gish, James Rennie.

*BROADWAY. With Bette Davis, in a small part.

Index